WALKING IN THE OCHILS, CAMPSIE FELLS AND LOMOND HILLS

About the Author

As a keen outdoor enthusiast, Patrick Baker spends the majority of his free time walking, climbing or scrambling in the Scottish hills. This passion for the outdoors has led to several expeditions in major mountain ranges across Europe, but closer to home, time spent in the mountains of the West Highlands and the Cairngorms, and the hills of central Scotland, is an ongoing source of interest and enjoyment. Patrick lives with his wife in Edinburgh, where he works in the publishing industry.

WALKING IN THE OCHILS, CAMPSIE FELLS AND LOMOND HILLS

33 Walks in Scotland's Central Fells

by

Patrick Baker

2 POLICE SQUARE, MILNTHORPE, CUMBRIA LA7 7PY
www.cicerone.co.uk

A catalogue record for this book is available from the British Library.
All photographs are by the author except where stated otherwise.

DEDICATION
For my parents, Melvyn and Angela

Acknowledgements
I wish to thank the following people who have accompanied me on these routes: Andy Baker, Steve Owen, Chris Burton, Simon Gall, Andy and Clare Davis, Irene Kale and George Lupton. Thanks also to George Lupton and Joe Buchanan for the use of their photographs, and Gregor Hutton for the original map illustrations. Thanks to the Filmer family for technological back up. Many thanks to John and Noreen Young for all their advice and useful suggestions. Finally, I would like to thank my wife Jacqui for all her patience, ideas and support.

Advice to Readers
Readers are advised that while every effort is taken by the author to ensure the accuracy of this guidebook, changes can occur which may affect the contents. It is advisable to check locally on transport, accommodation, shops, etc., but even rights of way can be altered. Paths can be affected by forestry work, land-slip or changes of ownership.

The author would welcome information on any updates and changes sent through the publishers.

Front cover: The view from Dunmore, Campsie Fells

GRAHAM TISO LIMITED
TISO GLASGOW
129 BUCHANAN STREET
Tel No: 0141 248 4877
VAT Reg No: 917907105

Till number: 03 Receipt ID: 3171190

GS004 30-JUN-10 14:45

Style	Qty	Unit	Amount
TISO-CICE-1058047	1	10.00	10.00
Ochils Campsie Fells Lomond			
NO COLOUR - N-A			

	Amount Due:	10.00
Tendered	CASH	10.00

VAT Type	Net	VAT	Gross
0 ZERO VAT RATED	10.00	0.00	10.00

Outlet: 01 Register 03 Receipt ID: 3131180

40055 30-JUN-01 14:42

Style	QTY	Unit	Amount
1120-CICE-1029041	1	10.00	10.00

Quartz crystal Felis Fondou

NO COLOUR - N-N

		Amount Due:	10.00
	CASH	Tendered	10.00

VAT TYPE	NET	VAT	GROSS
0 ZERO VAT	10.00	0.00	10.00

DATED

CONTENTS

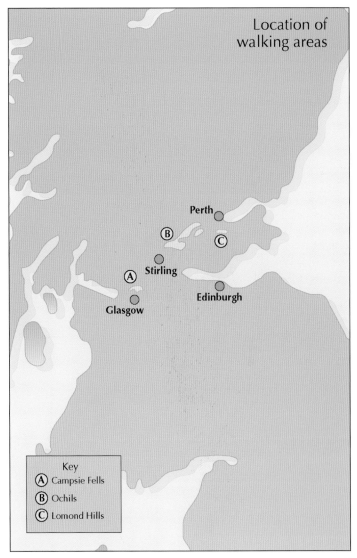

Location of walking areas

Perth

(B)

(C)

Stirling

(A)

Glasgow

Edinburgh

Key
(A) Campsie Fells
(B) Ochils
(C) Lomond Hills

Viewpoint from just below Benarty Hill (Walk 33)

INTRODUCTION

AREA GUIDE

The Ochils, Campsie Fells and Lomond Hills form a prominent band of high ground across the central belt of Scotland, providing a dramatic backdrop to the nearby cities of Glasgow, Edinburgh and Perth. Overlooked by many walkers on their way to larger hills in the north, these three ranges provide uniquely wild, challenging and beautiful walks literally on the doorstep of many towns and cities. Ironically, it is perhaps their proximity to these major areas of population which means that although they are some of most accessible wild areas in the country, these hills remain a relatively uncrowded oasis for walkers.

Formed from predominantly igneous rock, each of the ranges shows signs of volcanic creation, perhaps the most obvious indicators being the hills of Dumgoyne, Dumyat and West and East Lomond, whose conical shapes offer distinctive and appealing walks. The other main geological influence is glaciation, which has smoothed away rock to give characteristically broad, plateaued ridges and summits into which burns have gouged steep glens, creating precipitous gorges and waterfalls, in particular on the southern escarpment of the Ochils. The undulating nature of most of the hills is sharply contrasted by some large and spectacular crags and cliffs, most notably the breathtaking Corrie of Balglass in the Campsie Fells, and interesting quartz dolerite intrusions along the west-facing Lomond Hills.

Collectively the three ranges combine a rich mixture of distinct neighbouring habitats, ranging from: montane moorland, ancient and managed forestry, deep lochs and reservoirs, fast-flowing burns and meandering rivers, to rocky crags and fertile carseland. The walker is thus treated to flora and fauna in greater abundance and of greater accessibility than in many of the larger, more remote ranges of Scotland.

This guide offers a mixture of routes, including many popular peaks such as Ben Cleuch, Meikle Bin and West Lomond, as well as areas that are well off the beaten track. The walks have been chosen to reflect the diverse landscape that exists in these ranges, and affords as much importance to smaller peaks and lower-level walks as it does to larger hills and high traverses. Several of the walks include peaks known as 'Donalds' – hills in lowland Scotland over 2000ft that have a drop of 100ft

Evening sun on the Ochils

on all sides. They are named after Percy Donald, who compiled the original list of these hills.

While some walks are justifiably popular and lined with obvious tracks and paths, walkers are also encouraged to explore routes following the natural lines of ridges and glens where few or no paths exist, so that the guide not only gives details for enjoying some classic routes, but also acts as a starting point for linking and creating endless combinations of different routes. The majority of walks included are circular, and wherever possible start from a suitable place to park a car.

FLORA

Human intervention has altered the landscape in this area from almost completely woodland-covered hills hundreds of years ago, to what is now largely characterised by either grassy plateaued peaks colonised by sheep and livestock, or high, heather-strewn moorland and peat bogs.

At lower levels the slopes are often covered with **gorse** and **broom**, which produce large, vibrant patches of yellow as the plants flower from spring into summer. **Bracken** also proliferates on the lower slopes, providing excellent cover for birds and mammals, as well as enriching seasonal colours as it turns from lush green in summer to deeper browns in autumn, perfectly complementing the purple flowering of the dominant local **heather, ling**.

Ancient or regenerated natural woodland is also found, mainly on the lower reaches of the hills, in

Heather in bloom

particular on the steep-sided glens of the Ochils and Campsie Fells, where trees that would previously have been felled for fuel or industrial purposes are now assured regenerative protection from sheep and deer by enclosed fencing. Fine examples of these pockets of predominantly deciduous woodland can be seen at Dollar Glen, Mill Glen, Alva Glen and Menstrie Glen in the Ochils, and Campsie Glen and Fin Glen in the Campsie Fells. Amongst the most recognisable trees to be seen are: **oak**, **birch**, **ash**, **sycamore**, **rowan**, **horse chestnut**, **beech**, **elm**, **larch** and **Scots pine**.

Commercial afforestation has also played a conspicuous and controversial role in changing the appearance of these hills, with unmistakable areas of densely packed coniferous forestry (mainly **spruce**) evident from almost anywhere in each of the three ranges. The largest and highest plantation of this kind is to be found completely encircling Carron Valley Reservoir and almost reaching the summit of the Campsie Fells' second largest hill, Meikle Bin. There is also afforestation of a different kind in several areas south of Glen Devon in the Ochils, where the Woodland Trust has secured large areas of hillside to reintroduce native species of tree.

On a smaller scale, there is a profusion of flowering plants from early spring through to early autumn. Flowers such as **snowdrops** provide brightness early in the year, after which the short-lived **bluebell** and the **forget-me-not** produce spectacular eruptions of blue under the forest canopy. In summer, on relatively dry hilltops, flowers including the

Wild pansy

Forget-me-not in bloom in the Ochils

harebell, **meadow buttercup**, **white clover**, and the beautiful **wild pansy**, can be seen in abundance amongst grasses such as **sheep's fescue**, **wavy hair grass** and **mat grass**. The fluffy white fruiting heads of **cotton grass** are also a particularly common summer sight on high walks, and a good indicator of boggy areas, where pretty **bog asphodel** and the carnivorous **sundew** also thrive in these damper conditions. The western end of the Ochils supports one of the largest national populations of the rare, **sticky catchfly flower**, which can be found on the slopes of Dumyat and in Menstrie Glen. Scotland's national flower, the thistle, also makes sporadic appearances, usually in the form of the common **spear thistle** which flowers in late summer.

MAMMALS

Even the briefest period of time spent in these hills will lead to an encounter with wildlife in some shape or form, adding a rewarding dimension to a day's walk. The largest animals to be found are deer. While herds of **red deer** can occasionally be spotted in the Carron Valley between the Campsie Fells and Fintry Hills, the smaller and more solitary **roe deer** is more likely to be seen. Habitually shy, roe deer are normally only seen at a distance as they move stealthily between bracken thickets and woodland brush. A useful indicator of this elusive animal's presence is the telltale 'roe ring' – a repetition of cloven tracks found around a solitary tree or bush in summer, left as part of the deer's mating ritual.

Apart from the **fox**, which generally prefers the cover of night to hunt, the area's largest carnivore is the **stoat**. Quick and agile, it is a cunning and ferocious hunter, most likely to be seen in pursuit of **rabbits**. The stoat's black-tipped tail distinguishes it from its smaller relative, the **weasel**. Along with a non-native cousin, the **black mink**, these three are the most common members of the Mustelid family in the region.

Smaller animals that make up the diet of carnivores, such as the **wood mouse**, **vole** and **shrew**, are all to be found, but are less likely to be seen than larger prey such as rabbits or the **brown hare**. Often initially mistaken for a rabbit or a brown hare when not in its distinctive all-white (except for black tips on the ears) winter coat, the native **mountain hare** or **blue hare** can occasionally be seen high in the hills, generally at dusk and dawn, where it feeds on dwarf shrubs and shelters in 'forms' in heather.

Despite being displaced from much of its native habitat by the larger, non-native **grey squirrel**, the indigenous **red squirrel** is still seen in many of the areas of woodland covered in this guide, in particular in the east of the Ochils and Forrestmill, and the Carron Valley Forest. Generally harder to spot than the larger and bolder grey, the red squirrel spends more time in the tree-tops and prefers predominantly coniferous woodland, where its diet consists mainly of seeds retrieved

from cones, with the distinctive, roughly gnawed cone remnants left as evidence of its feeding activity.

By far the most ubiquitous animal to be encountered is the **sheep**. As a vital part of the agricultural livelihood of these hills, walkers should take every possible precaution not to upset sheep (further advice about behaviour in the hills is found in the Access and the Environment section).

BIRDS

The vast number of migrant or year-round-resident birds likely to be seen in the area is too large to list in this introduction, but many interesting species will inevitably be spotted in the course of a walk.

The heather-strewn and grassy moorlands typical of the higher areas provide a perfect habitat for birds such as the **skylark**, **grouse** and **curlew** to feed, nest and breed in. If these birds are inadvertently disturbed from their ground-based activities, they will fly away making loud – and in the case of the **grouse**, startling, – alarm calls. The **wheatear** is also a common sight on high tops. This inquisitive bird often appears to accompany the walker during the summer months, flying ahead along drystone dykes, and displaying striking white tail feathers while producing a distinctively harsh 'tack, tack' call. But the most constant year-round companion of all is probably the **buzzard**, whose unmistakable 'meowing' call is a certain indicator that this large bird is circling somewhere high in the sky overhead, on the look out for either live prey or carrion. With so much prey available, the hills also support many other raptors, including the **kestrel**, **merlin**, **peregrine falcon**, **tawny** and **short-eared owls**, as well as small numbers of **red kites**, which can occasionally be seen in the Sheriffmuir area of the Ochils.

The remarkably successful reintroduction of breeding **ospreys** in Scotland means that sightings of these birds, typically circling above fish-stocked lochs and reservoirs, are relatively common in the summer. Good places to spot osprey are the Carron Valley Reservoir, North Third Reservoir and Castle Hill Reservoir.

As many of the routes in this guide initially pass through woodland, a wide variety of birds will often be seen and heard at the start and end of walks. Smaller species such as **tits**, **warblers**, **chaffinch**, **siskin** and even **goldcrest** are found in abundance in wooded areas, along with other less obvious examples such as the **treecreeper** and **wren**. Although rarely seen, the elusive **green woodpecker** is also a resident of many of the wooded glens in the Ochils and Campsies, in particular Dollar Glen, where in spring its loud and distinctive 'yaffle' call can often be heard.

Along the fast-flowing burns of many of the wooded glens, birds such as **dippers** and **grey wagtails** can be

spotted feeding on insects and larvae near the water's edge.

WEATHER

The hills covered in this guide stretch right across the central belt of Scotland, and as such there is good scope for choosing routes to take advantage of the varied weather conditions in different areas. For instance, poor weather in the Campsie Fells in the west may often coincide with a clear day in the Lomond Hills further east, and vice versa. The Campsie Fells generally experience more rain than the Lomond Hills, but many of the routes described in the Campsies will avoid the prevailing winds that the higher tops of the Ochils are exposed to, which can be particularly hard and cold in winter.

Walking is possible year round, with May, June and September generally providing the clearest and most pleasant days out. The coldest months are January and February, when snow is most likely to fall, especially on the high peaks of the Ochils. However, a sharp frost during winter can bring the welcome benefit of hardening otherwise soft, boggy ground.

Hill fog is reasonably common, and seems to be more frequent during low-pressure conditions in late spring and late autumn. Quite often a mist will prevail in the Forth Valley long after the sun has burnt away the cloud on the Ochils, creating spectacular

Storm clouds seen from the Lomond Hills (Walks 30 and 32) © George Lupton

temperature inversions where walkers may find themselves above a sea of cloud. Weather conditions at the top of hills need to be considered, as they may be much more extreme than the seemingly temperate conditions at the start of a walk.

HISTORY

Over the centuries the hills covered in this guide have been a defining factor in the lives of the inhabitants of the area. Equally, people have greatly determined the appearance of the hills as they are today. The many once-forested hillsides and summits have been cleared over the years to provide fuel and building materials, and the actual shape of the hills has been altered through mining, quarrying and mill-related activities.

Amongst the oldest and most obvious signs of man in the landscape are the numerous remains of Iron Age forts, which can found across all three ranges. Mainly built on the most prominent and defendable hills, many forts took advantage of the steep slopes of volcanic plugs such as Dumyat, and in particular East Lomond, where the site of an Iron Age fort encompasses the entire summit. Other notable forts can be found on Benarty Hill, Easter Downhill and Dunmore, where narrow trenches (sometimes with stone remains) surrounding earthern mounds let the unsuspecting walker know that they are standing on an historic site and not just another summit.

Perhaps the most ancient and beguiling place in the region is the line of standing stones at Sheriffmuir in the Ochils. Supposedly once the rallying point for William Wallace's troops before the Battle of Stirling Bridge in 1297, and for the Jacobite Army before the Battle of Sheriffmuir in 1715, the five perfectly aligned stones (of which now only one remains standing) retain a mystery of purpose, and certainly date back to a much more ancient people.

Without doubt, the most striking historic building in the area is Castle Campbell. Situated on the high ground at the head of Dollar Burn, in between the gorges carved by the Burn of Care and the Burn of Sorrow, this castle has one of the most beautiful settings in the country. Originally called Castle Gloom, the Clan Campbell acquired it in the 15th century, and in the 17th century, under a royal decree, changed its name to Castle Campbell. Other notable historic buildings seen or passed on some of the walks include the remains of Fintry Castle, Glendevon Castle, Falkland Palace and Loch Leven Castle – the one-time prison of Mary Queen of Scots.

As well as their strategic importance, there is also evidence of the hills being used as a place of refuge for local people. The Covenantor Hole below Dunmore in the Campsies, and John Knox's Pulpit in the Lomond Hills, are likely sites of Presbyterian conventicles held in secret during the late 17th century, to escape the period's religious persecution, dubbed the 'Killing Times'.

The fluctuating economic significance of the hills, in particular the Ochils, is also closely linked with human history. During the Industrial Revolution the fast-flowing burns from the steep southern escarpment of the Ochils supplied the ideal method of powering the many textile mills that came into existence in the collectively named 'Hillfoot' towns of Menstrie, Tillicoultry and Alva. At the height of production, towards the last quarter of the 19th century, the Hillfoots was the second largest wool-producing area in Scotland, with over 1500 people directly employed in the textile industry in the town of Alva alone. Fine examples of mill houses are the Clock Mill, ideally located at the bottom of Mill Glen, and the large Strude building in Alva.

Heavy industry was present in the Ochils, however, before the advent of textile production. The discovery of silver at the beginning of the 18th century sparked some large-scale mining operations. At their most prolific they were producing silver to the value of £4000 per week from the largest known deposit of silver ore in Great Britain. Other minerals such as coal and copper have also been heavily exploited in the Ochils, and the hills themselves bear the marks of these mining activities, in particular the numerous mines-shaft openings found in and around the aptly named Silver Glen.

PRACTICALITIES

The walks are divided into three sections, one for each range of hills, and each section opens with an introduction to the area. All the route descriptions begin with a summary of information, along with an **overview** of what can be expected on the walk, including any significant details concerning terrain and navigation. The summary includes the **distance**, **height gain** and **approximate time** required for the walk (the time estimated for each walk is calculated at a walking speed of 5km an hour, using Naismith's Rule for ascent, and does not include time taken for breaks), as well as the required **map** and a **difficulty rating**.

The maps in the guide are from the OS 1:50,000 Landranger series, but **it is highly advisable to also carry the relevant OS 1:25,000 Explorer or Harvey's 1:25,000 maps** (identified in the summary at the start of the walk), as many routes require intricate map referencing unavailable on the larger 1:50,000 maps. The difficulty rating takes into account navigation, terrain and time spent on the hill, and ranges from 1, which is an easily manageable route such as Walk 24, Dungoil in the Campsie Fells, to 4 for routes such as Walk 20, the Round of Nine in the

Ochils, which involves long distances, some difficult terrain underfoot and potentially complicated navigating.

A basic level of ability in macronavigating is assumed, as is the understanding of grid references, map orientation, gradients, map symbols and estimation of distances. For more challenging routes the ability to use a compass in setting and walking on bearings is crucial, as are micronavigational skills involved in timing and pacing distances.

Quite often route descriptions will refer to '**attack points**'. These are obvious features that are aimed for en route to a less visible destination point near the 'attack point'. Many of the routes also use obvious linear features in the landscape – such as a burn, the edge of a forest or a fenceline – as useful 'navigational handrails' that lead the walker on to the next obvious feature on a route.

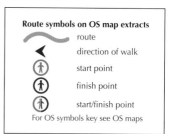

Route symbols on OS map extracts

	route
◄	direction of walk
(🚶)	start point
(🚶)	finish point
(🚶)	start/finish point

For OS symbols key see OS maps

A view of Dumgoyne in the Campsie Fells (Walk 21)

PLANNING AND PREPARATION

An element of risk is inherent in all the hills and wild places visited in this guide. Fortunately, **careful planning** and **preparation** can minimise potential risks, and the hills can be enjoyed safely and respectfully.

Before setting out, careful consideration should be given to whether the demands of a particular walk can be met by the **fitness**, **equipment**, **experience** and **skills** of those undertaking it. For example, it would be foolish for a walker with only basic map reading skills to attempt a route through featureless terrain in poor visibility.

When a walk has been selected, a 'route card' (a simple description of the route to be taken, along with an estimated time to arrive back and a note of the number of people in the group) should be left with someone who can anticipate your return.

Weather conditions should also be taken into account before starting out – obtain accurate, up-to-date local forecasts where possible. The route descriptions assume summer conditions prevail, but our maritime climate means that extreme weather is possible at any time of the year, and it should be assumed that a variety of conditions may occur in one day. When planning a walk the effects of weather should factored into the demands of the route, as strong winds and driving rains can be both energy sapping and demoralising, although hot and still days may have equally debilitating effects. **Clothing** and **equipment** should also be planned in advance to match the prevailing and expected conditions.

As well as being prepared with **essential equipment** (listed in the section below), some **dietary preparation** before and during a walk will be of benefit. The complex carbohydrates in starchy foods such as pasta, rice and wholemeal bread take longer to be broken down into an energy-giving form, so these are excellent for releasing energy evenly over longer periods, and are best consumed some time before a walk.

On the hill, a mix of different food groups will result in a sustained release of energy. Some typical foods to be packed in the rucksack could consist of those high in carbohydrates and fat, such as **peanut butter wholemeal sandwiches**, as well as those that supply natural sugars, such as **dried fruit**, proteins from **seeds** and **nuts**, and quick-release energy foods such as **chocolate**.

It is also important to replace the large amounts of fluid lost from the body during hillwalking. Burns and rivers are encountered on almost every walk in this guide, but the large amount of livestock found in most areas means that water collected during a walk may well be contaminated, so it is essential for enough water (1–1.5 litres is as an initial guide for an average-length walk) to be carried and consumed throughout a walk, with the principle of drinking 'small amounts often' to avoid the effects of dehydration.

ESSENTIAL EQUIPMENT

Appropriate **clothing** for the conditions likely to be experienced is key to an enjoyable and safe day's walking. Scotland is subject to the fickle nature of our climate more so than many

An excellent viewpoint along Endrick Water from Dunmore (Walk 26)

other areas of Britain, so even in summer, clothing needs to be able to adapt to sudden changes in weather. Despite recent innovations in the use of single, multipurpose garments, the most reliable method of combating changeable conditions is the **layering principle**, allowing the walker to achieve insulation and warmth, as well as protection from the elements, by combining different layers of clothing for specific purposes.

For the base layer, next to the skin, synthetic material such as polypropylene provides good insulation while transferring or 'wicking' perspiration away from the skin through to the layers of the outer garments. (Cotton t-shirts have the opposite effect – of storing moisture – and are thus unsuitable for colder conditions where they chill the body easily.) On top of the base layer, thicker, insulating garments, such as a fleece or woollen jumper, should be worn for heat retention, after which the outer layer or 'shell' should be a waterproof and wind-proof fabric that is also breathable, allowing moisture to escape to the outside.

The layering principle is relevant for both summer and winter conditions, as layers are added or removed to adapt to the work-rate (and heat generation) while walking, and the external weather conditions experienced. Other items to be carried year-round are a warm hat and gloves, while in summer a wide-brimmed hat is essential to protect against the sun. In addition to the clothing worn on the day, it is advisable to carry a warm, lightweight fleece inside a waterproof bag in the rucksack.

Choice of **footwear** generally comes down to personal preference, but the mixed terrain encountered on these walks means that proper hill-walking boots rather than shoes or trainers are required. Assuming non-winter walking conditions apply, the boots should be reasonably flexible, waterproof with a bellowed tongue, have good ankle support but allow for enough movement over different gradients, and have a sole with grips that are thick enough for moving over rocky ground. To avoid blisters, new boots should be 'broken in' gradually before being used on long walks.

Personal equipment should be carried in a **well-fitting rucksack**, with items that need to be kept dry stored in a waterproof liner, such as a plastic bin bag. Amongst the essential items to be carried on any of these walks are:

- a survival bag
- torch
- whistle
- map
- compass
- waterproof map case
- first aid kit
- mobile phone
- pencil and paper
- food and water
- spare fleece.

Walking in larger groups or more testing conditions may also require a group shelter to be carried, but as with any walk, a balance should be struck between necessity and the weight of items carried. A particularly useful piece of equipment is **adjustable walking poles**, which can not only be used to reduce the strain on legs and knees while walking, but are also very handy for judging the conditions of soft and boggy terrain ahead.

HILLCRAFT

Despite being relatively low compared to the larger ranges in the Scottish Highlands, the hills covered in this guide present challenges that require similar levels of skills and experience – or 'hillcraft' – to those that would be needed in more mountainous regions. Typical characteristics such as high areas of featureless terrain, steep slopes and occasional large crags, will at times require confidence in personal ability, and good judgement.

Navigation

Competent navigation is the primary skill required for anyone wishing to enjoy safe hillwalking. While navigational skills will take time to master and maintain, familiarity with map reading undoubtedly helps in selecting walks, and enhances confidence, enjoyment and safety on the hills. The route descriptions in this

guide assume a basic level of navigational understanding (detailed in the How to Use This Guide section). Courses, books and spending time on the hills with competent friends are all good ways to begin learning navigation.

Sickness and Injury

Common sense, planning and good navigation should mean most difficult situations on the hill are avoided. However, in situations where an individual hillwalker or a member of a hillwalking party are immobilised due to sickness or injury, some basic procedures will ensure circumstances do not get out of control.

- Firstly, find some shelter in the immediate vicinity (which in these hills may be difficult). Even the most minimal cover from wind and rain, such as a peat hag or drystone dyke, will help.

- Maintain body heat by adding any extra clothes and climbing inside a survival bag (and then the group shelter if one is available).

- Treat medical conditions or injuries as well as you can using the first aid kit, considering these as an on-going concern. Focus also on maintaining personal and group morale.

- If a signal is available on a mobile phone, call for help from the Mountain Rescue services by first dialling 999 and asking for the police. Be ready to inform

Mountain Rescue of your location, ideally by giving a six-figure grid reference. Mountain Rescue may also need to know details such as the number of walkers in the party, any medical conditions or injuries sustained, a description of the surrounding area, and the time and location at which the walk began. If no phone or signal is available, the above details should be written down and given to the most able person if they are in a position to seek help. **The importance of leaving a route card is obvious (in particular for the individual walker) when emergency situations arise**.

- Once help has been requested it is important to stay at the exact location. Signal for help using the recognised rescue code of six long blasts with a whistle and/or six flashes of a torch every minute, listening out for three whistles or flashes as a response from the rescuers. Continue using the code until you have been reached by Mountain Rescue.

An appropriate first aid kit and a basic knowledge of first aid will help to relieve some uncomfortable minor injuries. **Blisters** are perhaps the most common problem experienced by hillwalkers, but can be avoided by wearing well-fitting boots that have been broken in over a period of time.

If blisters occur it is best to treat them as soon as possible. In the early stages of a blister, applying Vaseline will help reduce the friction that creates sore points on the soft tissue of the foot. Alternatively, rather than bursting any swelling it is preferable to simply cover the blister with a plaster or other dressing to avoid further rubbing.

Other common complaints such as **sprains** are also largely preventable with appropriate footwear and careful placement of the feet while walking. Inevitably, when sprains do occur they are painful, and severely restrict the pace of walking, so providing support to the injured area by snugly binding it with gaffer tape (carried in the first aid kit or taped around a walking pole) is often the ideal treatment. Walking poles are extremely useful in relieving pressure on sprains and twists.

Less preventable and more difficult to deal with, **fractures** are often the result of falls or slips. Fractures to the legs or ankles will almost certainly require rescue assistance, while fractures to the arms or wrists may well be supported by creating a sling from a triangular bandage kept in the first aid kit, or by improvising with an item of clothing.

Perhaps the most serious medical conditions to be aware of result from environmental factors affecting the body's core temperature. Walkers who are unprepared for the effects of heat loss, due to inadequate clothing

Walkers on Andrew Gannel Hill with King's Seat in the background (Walks 11 and 20)

or a lack of equipment to cope with an enforced stop, may quickly become susceptible to **hypothermia**. The very serious effects of hypothermia are felt in a relatively short space of time and are initially hard to recognise. Feelings of fatigue, listlessness and irritability are some of the vague symptoms common at the onset of 'exposure', which if not spotted early on can quickly spiral into the later stages of hypothermia. Thankfully, good planning and preparation should eliminate most circumstances where hypothermia may arise.

As with hypothermia, **heat exhaustion** is also easily preventable, but if left untreated can also lead to more serious conditions. Heat exhaustion occurs gradually due to a loss of water and salts from the body as a result of vigorous exercise in warm, still temperatures. The body becomes less able to dissipate heat effectively, leading to feelings of fatigue, light-headedness and muscle cramps. Heat exhaustion is best prevented by a regular intake of liquid and by regulating body temperature while walking. However, at the first symptoms the walker should seek shade and rest, take on board fluids, and eat sweet and salty foods.

The effects of **sunburn** should also be prevented on hot days by covering exposed skin with clothing or sunscreen, which should always be carried in the first aid kit in the summer months. Other recommended items in the first aid kit may include:

- crepe bandages
- lint dressing
- triangular bandage
- plasters
- blister kit
- wound closure strips
- saline wash
- disposable gloves
- antiseptic wipes
- gaffer tape
- scissors
- emergency high-energy food.

24

ACCESS AND THE ENVIRONMENT

Most land in Scotland and the areas covered in this guide is privately owned. The long-standing tradition of freedom of access to the hills in Scotland was formalised through legislation in February 2005, giving hillwalkers statutory rights of responsible access within the guidelines of the Scottish Outdoor Access Code.

Scottish Outdoor Access Code
The main points of the code relevant to responsible hillwalking are summarised below.
- Take personal responsibility for your own actions.
- Respect people's privacy and peace of mind.
- Help land managers and others to work safely and effectively.
- Care for your environment.
- Keep your dog under proper control.

The guidelines of the code should translate into responsible action, with an awareness of the particular environment walkers find themselves in.

Some specific advice that hillwalkers should consider for the areas covered in this guide is as follows.
- Minimising disturbance to sheep, especially during lambing season (March–May). Dogs should be kept on leads at all times near sheep and efforts should always be made not to unduly upset them.

- Carry a plastic bag in your pocket to collect any litter you see. Don't just take your own litter home with you; walking past the litter left by the ignorant few is almost as bad as dropping it in the first place.

- Be aware of the grouse-shooting season (12 August – 10 December). Also be aware of work carried out near farms and on forestry tracks, observing any reasonable request from land managers. It is respectful to ask permission to use the land if the landowner is met, and they will often be able to give you good advice on areas to avoid or good routes.

- A lot of the routes in this guide cross fences. Wherever possible use the stiles provided or walk around fences. If a fence does need to be crossed, avoid applying weight to the fence, in particular by taking off heavy packs before crossing.

- Stick to paths when possible, keeping to the middle of the path to avoid further widening it.

- Minimise the environmental impact of your walking by using public transport or one car for transporting several friends to the start of a route.

- Do not disturb wildlife or the environment by picking plants/flowers or interfering with the habitats of birds and animals.

25

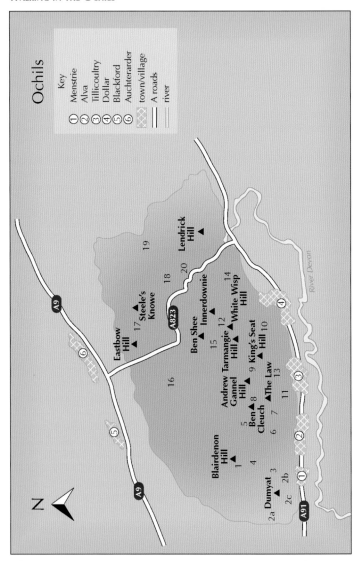

THE OCHILS

Rising abruptly from the carseland of the Forth Valley, the southern escarpment of the Ochils forms one of the most dramatic and distinctive profiles of any range of hills in the country. The steep southern slopes and crags have been gouged by fast-flowing burns to create some breathtaking gorge-like glens that lead onto broad, whalebacked ridges and summits.

The highest peak, Ben Cleuch, sits curiously beyond immediate view from the bottom of the hills, but is the main spinal massif that branches out to several main ridges that can be linked in many different combinations of walks. For instance, the popular Ben Cleuch Circuit (**Walk 8**), which is a fine walk in its own right, can easily be extended to include neighbouring peaks such as Andrew Gannel Hill, Ben Buck (**Walk 5**), Craighorn and even Bengengie Hill, yet still remain a pleasant circular route.

Separate smaller walks should also not be overlooked, with Dumyat (**Walk 2**) providing remarkably different approaches from three directions, the most exciting being the route up the cavernous gully of Warlock Glen (**Walk 2C**).

Other shorter routes such as the Nebit (**Walk 6**), Wood Hill (**Walk 7**) or Kirk Burn Glen (**Walk 13**) are also an excellent opportunity to explore in detail some of the unique terrain and features of the southern escarpment.

As the Ochils slope away gently towards the Strathearn Valley from their highest peaks in the south, the interior landscape changes from predominantly grassy tops to a mixture of blanket bog, tussocked grass and heather. While the peaks also become less defined, the sense of solitude is much increased, and some particularly fine and undisturbed routes include the Innerdownie Ridge (**Walk 12**), Blairdennon (**Walk 1**) and Steele's Knowe (**Walk 17**). The longest routes, such as the old drovers' route from Tillicoultry to Blackford (**Walk 11**) and the Round of Nine (**Walk 20**) provide rewarding traverses across the range.

Access is gained to the hills on the southern escarpment from the Hillfoot towns of Menstrie, Alva, Tillicoultry and Dollar, while the interior and northern routes are best accessed from Glen Devon.

WALK 1
Blairdenon Circuit

Distance	9.8km
Height gain	372m
Time	2hr 30min
Difficulty rating	3
Maps	OS Landranger 57 (1:50,000)
	OS Landranger 58 (1:50,000)
	OS Explorer 366 (1:25,000)
	Harvey's Map – Ochil Hills (1:25,000)
Start point	Sheriffmuir Road (GR827021)

The westernmost Donald in the Ochils, Blairdenon, is also the most remote. As such it is often only visited as a supplementary peak to routes started from the southern escarpment. This little-known and pleasant circular route, however, approaches the peak from the historic moorland of Sheriffmuir on the western reaches of the range. Conveniently starting and finishing near the solitary Sheriffmuir Inn, the route forms a long horseshoe around picturesque Glen Tye. Defined paths are absent for the majority of walk, but the going underfoot is unchallenging except for some boggy ground at Menstrie Moss.

A lack of paths and any real navigational features on the first half of the walk means that in poor visibility it is only suitable for those skilled in micronavigation.

The walk starts from the Sheriffmuir Road at the western edge of the Ochils. Parking is available off the road just down from the Sheriffmuir Inn, next to a row of trees and a drystone dyke (GR827021). This historic area of the Ochils is near the site of the Battle of Sheriffmuir, where in 1715 the Jacobite Army led by the Earl of Mar clashed with Hanoverian forces in a bloody and equally incompetently fought encounter.

Looking towards the picturesque Glen Tye from Sherrifmuir

To start the walk, go through a dilapidated metal gate into the heather-strewn field opposite where the car is parked and take the immediately obvious quad tracks in an eastward direction. The quad tracks soon melt into a narrow and barely visible path which essentially takes the line of least resistance through the heather, wending its way east for 600m from the gate to arrive at the obvious end of Glen Tye. ▸

On reaching the bottom of Glen Tye, cross the drystone dyke and descend to cross the Old Wharry Burn, just below where it is joined by a smaller burn, and ascend up the bank on the south side of the glen. Without a path, head towards the obvious plantation, passing it on the northern side just south of the glen, reaching a small burn shortly afterwards. Cross the small burn and begin to ascend the gentle slopes of Little Hunt Hill by moving southeasterly and away from Glen Tye. The going underfoot is full of small tussocks, but fairly easy. The small, flat and unmarked summit of Little Hunt Hill (421m) provides good views immediately over Sheriffmuir and west to the Gargunnock Hills.

Leaving Little Hunt Hill, navigation can become difficult in poor weather. Head easterly from the summit to cross a fence, entering temporarily into some soggy

To the left at this point is a set of almost perfectly linearly aligned standing stones, visible by the only remaining upright stone, 'Wallace's Stone', so called as it was apparently often used as the meeting place for William Wallace's army. The placement of these stones, however, almost certainly predates Wallace's time.

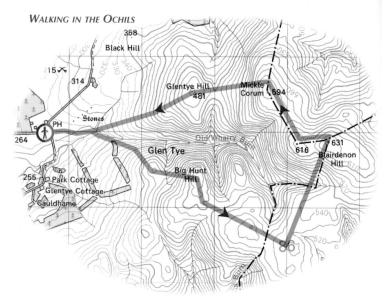

terrain before ascending steadily to the oblong and unmarked top of Big Hunt Hill (520m). A lack of any useful navigational features at this point means that close attention to macronavigation is required in clear weather, and precise micronavigation must be used in poor visibility to stay on route.

Head southeasterly from the top of Big Hunt Hill to the spot-height marked 496m at GR849009 in between the start of two burns (taking a bearing to this point is advisable even in good weather). Begin to ascend gradually from this point, heading to the spot-height marked 541m (Explorer) at GR855007, and continue east to the fenceline at Menstrie Moss. Here the terrain becomes quite boggy in parts, but navigation becomes easier as a faint path parallels the fence northwards, descending to a small burn (after crossing a fence) and then ascending all the way to Blairdenon Hill (still roughly following the fence). The flat, featureless top of Blairdenon (631m) is probably the most uninspiring in the Ochils, so there is not much reason to linger on the unmarked summit.

Cross over to the north side of the fence and take the vague, grassy path next to the fence that heads southwesterly towards Greenforet Hill. Just before reaching Greenforet there is a humble memorial cairn with a small white cross, planted amongst several pieces of twisted and rusting metal. The sobering memorial marks a more recent part of Ochils history, when numerous aircraft crashed over the hills during the Second World War. The worst occasion was 18 January 1943, when three Spitfires flying in formation crashed in the Ochils, killing two of the pilots.

After the memorial the path bends around without actually reaching Greenforet summit and descends towards the col before Mickle Corum. ▸ Ascend gradually from the col to Mickle Corum summit (594m) and cross the fence to reach the obvious cairn to enjoy perhaps the best vantage point west in the range.

Descend almost due west from the cairn for 700m, again without a path, to reach a broad col, and proceed gently upwards in the same direction for a further 300m to the broad, unmarked top of Glentye Hill (481m). Change direction from Glentye Hill and descend in a roughly southwesterly direction, edging gradually closer to the Old Wharry Burn to eventually arrive back at the bottom of Glen Tye where this burn was originally crossed.

From here cross back over the burn and return to the start point near the Sheriffmuir Inn. (It is worth taking a swift diversion to Wallace's Stone and the four other linearly aligned stones.)

This is the best part of the walk, with great views north and west and a good view down Glen Tye from the col.

WALK 2
Dumyat Hill

The most distinctive hill in the Ochils range, Dumyat is a relatively small but undeniably handsome volcanic plug at the western corner of the southern escarpment. Its easy accessibility from a couple of car parking spots means that this is also the busiest hill in the range, and as such the main path up to its summit can become quite congested at times and is very badly eroded in parts. However, the three circular routes below aim to make the most of the differing approaches to this complex hill, and also avoid the main crowds.

A) An easy and quick route to the summit that circles back to the start point via the eastern flank of the hill

Distance	5km
Height gain	403m
Time	1hr 40min
Difficulty rating	1
Maps required	OS Landranger 57 (1:50,000)
	OS Landranger 58 (1:50,000)
	OS Explorer 366 (1:25,000)
	Harvey's Map – Ochil Hills (1:25,000)
Start point	Blairlogie car park (GR832968)

Head north from the car park up a few steps to the stile and cross the track to head directly onto the small path that ascends steeply for 10m through shrubs. This path proceeds to contour around the side of the hill westwards, squeezing through brambles and gorse bushes for a few hundred metres until it crosses a small burn in more open ground. The path becomes more established at this point and climbs parallel to the wooded burn, past the convergence of tributary burns, to cross one of these tributary burns after approximately 250m.

Ahead, the more visible path moving upwards into more craggy terrain is to be ignored. Instead, take the grassy route through bracken, keeping a small scree section under some small crags to the right, to shortly arrive at a gate. Once through the gate, continue on the obvious path as it rises to meet the very well-established path running east to west. Take this track east, reaching a stile at the boggy watershed for the Warroch Burn. ▸ Continue for a few more minutes to reach the summit of Dumyat (418m), marked on its rocky top by a cairn and a stone-filled beacon.

The exit route from the summit is not immediately clear, but the path begins just 10m or so northeast of the cairn and zigzags down before flattening to an obvious grassy route that continues southeasterly, reaching a farm track just after a fenced water-drainage area. Turn right at the farm track and descend along the track, passing some houses as the route swings round beneath the impressive south-facing crags of Dumyat until reaching the burn at Warlock Glen.

At this point, instead of passing through the gate and cattle-grid, turn up the path by the sign saying Dumyat Farm and cross the burn at the small footbridge. Continue along this path, with pleasant mixed woodland on the left, until you arrive back at the stile at Blairlogie car park.

At this point, the short diversion south to the top of Castle Law is worthwhile for a less crowded summit view.

33

B) An ambling and gradual route that follows the verdant and tranquil Menstrie Glen behind the back of Dumyat for the least busy ascent of the hill

Distance	6km
Height gain	403m
Time	1hr 50min
Difficulty rating	2
Maps required	OS Landranger 57 (1:50,000)
	OS Landranger 58 (1:50,000)
	OS Explorer 366 (1:25,000)
	Harvey's Map – Ochil Hills (1:25,000)
Start point	Menstrie (GR851971)

This section of the walk is perhaps the most pleasant, particularly in summer months when the sound of the slow-moving burn and the lush greenery of trees and bracken create a really tranquil environment.

From the A91 at the west end of Menstrie, take Park Road, turning at the Holly Tree pub. As the road curves around to the right (away from the scout hut) park near the line of cottages.

At the end of the cottages a track heads towards the start of the hill, with a sign marking footpath on the wooden telephone pole. Cross here at the stile and follow the broad farm track, passing over a metal stile at the first loop in the track. Stay on this track as it somewhat tediously loops its way higher then contours parallel to Menstrie Burn.

At GR848974 leave the main farm track and continue along the grassy path that remains parallel to Menstrie Burn. After approximately 600m through bracken and gorse bushes, on the narrow but distinct path, go through the farm gate and cross the burn on the footbridge 200m further on. The path then descends amongst hazel trees to run by the side of the burn, crossing footbridges at the Second, then Third Ichna Burns. ◄

At the Third Ichna Burn, pass through the metal gate, but ignore the obvious route across the wooden footbridge over the Menstrie Burn, instead heading right and

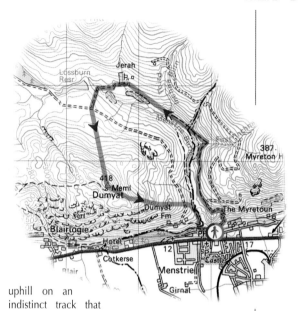

uphill on an indistinct track that leads into a grassy pasture with pleasant views back to the burn. As the path becomes less distinct and eventually fades completely, head towards the gate at the bottom end of the drystone dyke, now directly in view. Pass through the small gate and keep to the line of the fence on the left for 200m as it moves gradually uphill into another open meadow.

A line of trees at the end of the field comes into view with a ruined building at the top. Stay in the bottom third of the field and continue along to the line of trees to reach a metal gate at a stone bridge. Cross through the gate and over the bridge, at which point some care should be taken, as some of the wooden sleepers on the bridge are rather decayed.

After the bridge an obvious track loops around the ruins of a building to soon reach the crossing point at Loss Burn just below the reservoir. The track widens after the burn and ascends past the reservoir in the direction

35

*The view towards
the verdant
Menstrie Glen*

of Dumyat. Continue to head in the direction of the summit, leaving the track as it bends, moving onto the vague grassy path, which, while indistinct, can be followed all the way to the top.

Descend the summit via the same route as A), above, until you reach a farm track just after the fenced water-drainage area. At this point cross the track to pass over the stile diagonally opposite and continue descending on the clear path for another 5 minutes before reaching the metal gate and concrete steps that lead back on to the road. Turn left and pass the scout hut to return to the cottages and the start of the walk.

C) The most exciting route up Dumyat, heading up the cavernous gully of Warlock Glen between Castle Law and the main Dumyat summit

Distance	5km
Height gain	403m
Time	1hr 40min
Difficulty rating	2
Maps required	OS Landranger 57 (1:50,000)
	OS Landranger 58 (1:50,000)
	OS Explorer 366 (1:25,000)
	Harvey's Map – Ochil Hills (1:25,000)
Start point	Blairlogie car park (GR831968)

Head north from the car park up a few steps to the stile and onto the vehicle track. Turn right and walk along the track for 300m before moving off the track and onto the grassy bank on the left. Head up this bank without a path in between gorse

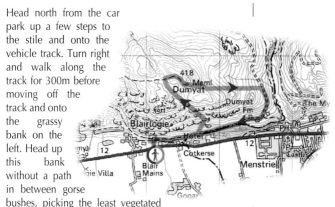

bushes, picking the least vegetated line of resistance in an upward diagonal slant, essentially heading towards the obvious groove of Warroch Burn.

Although a path is not really evident, the gully of Warlock Glen should become increasingly obvious, and soon a route should be found directly uphill parallel to the burn to enter in between the steep crags of the gully, which is easily one of the most impressive yet least explored features of the range. A faint path is picked up once fully inside the gully, and this crosses back and forth over the now small burn. At this point it is worth exploring some of the numerous nooks and crannies in the gully.

The path and the burn arrive into open and somewhat damp ground at the top of the gully just opposite Castle Law, the site of an Iron Age fort and also an excellent viewing point. Turn left to walk the short distance to Castle Law, or walk directly ahead (avoiding some fairly boggy ground), and on reaching the main path for Dumyat turn right and proceed along the path to shortly arrive at the summit after a very minor scramble. Exit from the hills and return to the car park via Route A), above.

WALK 3
Myreton Hill

Distance	4.6km
Height gain	370m
Time	1hr 30min
Difficulty rating	1
Maps required	OS Landranger 57 (1:50,000)
	OS Landranger 58 (1:50,000)
	OS Explorer 366 (1:25 000)
	Harvey's Map – Ochil Hills (1:25,000)
Start point	Menstrie (GR851971)

One of the less visited hills on the south face of the Ochils, Myreton Hill can be a refreshing alternative to more popular, crowded summits such as Dumyat and the Law. Although lacking the height of neighbouring peaks, the westward perspective of Dumyat and Menstrie Glen certainly justifies an exploration to this easily reached top. An easy circular walk that uses defined paths and tracks for the majority of the route.

From the A91 at the west end of Menstrie, take Park Road, turning at the Holly Tree pub. As the road curves around to the right (away from the scout hut) park near the line of cottages.

At the end of the cottages a track heads towards the hill, with a sign marking footpath on the wooden telephone pole. Cross here at the stile and follow the broad farm track, passing over a metal stile at the first loop in the track. Stay on this track as it somewhat tediously loops its way higher, then contours parallel to Menstrie Burn before rising in an easterly direction through a series of large boulders and knolls.

As the track bends at point GR854978, take the initially grassy path that leads off the main track and ascends up the grassy bank before disappearing. Now without a path, continue to ascend to the highest point, the top of the large knoll at GR856979. At this point the summit ridge of Myreton Hill comes into view.

Move towards the drystone dyke directly in view and ascend parallel to the dyke for 100m, crossing through a gate and reaching the summit ridge. At the point where the dyke bends, cross over it and move towards the obvious cairn for views down to Menstrie and Alva below, as well as west to the angular slopes of Dumyat and the curving, wooded progression of Menstrie Glen.

> Due to the easy vehicular access via the farm track and the comparatively few walkers on this section of the Ochils, this hill is often popular with paragliders, and on warm, windy days this cairn can be an excellent vantage point for watching them take off and soar on Myreton's thermal currents.

To reach the actual summit point for the hill, cross back over the dyke from the cairn, heading northwards for 200m to reach the unmarked summit. From the summit descend directly east without a clear path to reach the Lethen Burn, and follow this feature for approximately 550m to reach a path that intersects the burn.

Take this path and continue descending, over occasionally boggy ground, following it as it curves around the hill westwards, ignoring any paths that lead to Balquharn. The path soon becomes more defined through the open ground that is alive with rabbits, and levels out to contour above Myreton House.

Remain walking above the level of the buildings, soon arriving into fields with denser

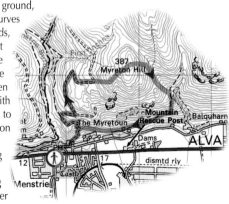

39

Paragliding from Myreton summit

shrubbery, and the path picks its way through gorse bushes, remaining parallel to the woodland 100m downhill on the left. Pass over a minor watercourse and a small ramshackle gate to enter another field, where the path becomes less distinct but the direction straight across remains the same, shortly arriving at a broad muddy track in front of a gate (ignoring a path leading downhill through the trees).

Pass through the gate (the gate slides across) and remain on this obvious track for a few minutes before arriving back at the metal stile and cattle-grid 100m from the start.

WALK 4
Bengengie Hill and Colsnaur Hill Circuit

Distance	9.5km
Height gain	565m
Time	2hr 50min
Difficulty rating	3
Maps required	OS Landranger 58 (1:50,000)
	OS Explorer 366 (1:25,000)
	Harvey's Map – Ochil Hills (1:25.000)
Start point	car park for Alva Glen (GR885975)

As well as providing some of the best views in the western Ochils, this challenging and interesting circular ridge walk also offers some quite unusual features along the way. A demanding ascent from Alva provides instant rewards – spectacular views and an immediate sense of height as well as quick access to the tops. The ridges are well defined, with the middle section of Bengengie Hill ridge being perhaps the narrowest ridge in the Ochils.

While the brief interior section of the route can at times be boggy, the walk is predominantly grassy and solid underfoot, and surprisingly craggy at times, with even the option of a small but satisfying scramble. Some flat sections without distinct paths mean basic navigation may be required on claggy days.

Instead of heading into Alva Glen, turn back towards the entrance of the car park at the north end of Alva and go through the gap in the stone wall to the right, crossing the top of the golf club car park to shortly arrive at some metal steps that lead into open ground at the end of the golf course.

From here turn sharply right and ascend uphill towards the wooden gate marked 'Rhodders Farm'. Once through the gate an obvious path picks its way between the gorse bushes, quickly gaining height and views above the golf course. Stay on this path as it ascends steeply, but before it begins to contour around the hill take the faint grassy track that leads steeply and directly northwest towards the obvious rocky outcrops of Wee Torry. This demanding section is also the first section of the lung-bursting Alva Run held every year in the second weekend of July and soon provides spectacular views down onto Alva.

On reaching the top of the gully, turn left onto Wee Torry for views that certainly justify this first section as a worth-while short walk in its own right, and are probably some of the best in the southern Ochils.

Contour around the lower crags of Wee Torry to the first interesting feature of the walk – a gully tucked slightly behind the main mound of the Wee Torry outcrop. This short, transverse gully walled by rocky outcrops on each side can assume an almost high-mountain presence when dusted with snow. ◄

Continue back along the path from the head of the gully onto the plateau of Torry. The path gradually fades as it merges into a surprising small boulder field adjacent to the head of the burn at Carnaughton Glen (approx. GR878982). In poor weather navigation at this point can become slightly tricky, as the terrain becomes more featureless, but continue in a northeasterly direction for approximately 750m to Mid Cairn, which is visible on a clear day.

*Alva Glen and Alva
from Wee Tory*

Once at Mid Cairn the path follows the obvious line of the ridge over firm ground for 1.5km to Bengengie Hill. With views left to the defined Colsnaur ridge and right to Alva Glen and the Craighorn and Ben Ever ridges, this is one of the most enjoyable sections of the walk. The middle section of the ridge, although hardly a knife edge, is by Ochil standards perhaps the narrowest area of ridge in the range.

Before long the remarkably craggy summit of Bengengie Hill comes into view. The tall southeastern escarpment, known locally as the Old Man, is a dramatic façade for a peak otherwise nestled in rolling moorland. The smaller crags also provide the perfect opportunity to reach the summit by means of an excellent, albeit short, scramble to the top (565m).

Leaving the summit of Bengengie in a northwesterly direction, the ridge changes to the flat, open moorland characteristic of the interior Ochils. Various tracks that head directly north towards Blairdenon Hill and eventually loop back are to be ignored. Instead, continue across the increasingly damp and tussocky open ground roughly towards a suitable crossing point above the watershed for the Balquharn Burn. (Note that during wet conditions it may be necessary to loop right above these boggy sections before access is gained to the Colsnaur ridge). Once on the ridge follow the drystone dyke (a useful linear feature in bad weather) to the summit of Colsnaur

Sights from the summit are the perhaps the best of the walk with excellent views towards Dumyat, the picturesque Lossburn Reservoir and beyond.

Hill (553m), marked with a cairn and pole. ◀ A large and comfortable trough underneath the cairn also provides excellent shelter and is a fine spot to lunch.

From Colsnaur summit easy navigation is maintained by following the fenceline that descends south off the hill until it becomes perpendicular with another fence. At this point follow the fence left towards Balquharn Burn, steeply descending to yet another interesting feature, a very small reservoir. At the gate for the reservoir ignore a path to the right that provides an exit to Menstrie, but continue across the reservoir walkway and ascend left on a faint path that heads northeasterly up the steep hill.

As the path eventually fades and the incline reduces (GR868983), head due east for just over 500km to the summit cairn of Craig Elsie. Heading in a northeasterly direction over some rocky ground, stay on the largely flat expanse for approximately 400m before turning back southeasterly onto Torry and retracing the original line of ascent to return to the start point.

Note that due to the steepness of the south-facing slopes it is advisable to make an exit from Wee Torry in the slightly more gradually inclined easterly or south-easterly direction that leads to the path above Alva Glen.

Scrambling on Bengengie Hill summit outcrop

WALK 5
Ben Cleuch via Ben Buck

Distance	9.5km
Height gain	721m
Time	3hr
Difficulty rating	3
Maps required	OS Landranger 58 (1:50,000)
	OS Explorer 366 (1:25,000)
	Harvey's Map – Ochil Hills (1:25,000)
Start point	car park for Alva Glen (GR885975)

A classic circular route to the Ochils' highest peak via the second highest point in the range, Ben Buck. Starting from the car park at Alva Glen the route initially approaches Ben Cleuch from the south, along the pleasant ascent of the Craighorn ridge, before curving around via Ben Buck, to reach Ben Cleuch from the north. The route exits the hills by the steep slopes of the Law, back through enjoyable woodland in Mill Glen and Wood Hill Wood. Apart from indistinct paths between Craighorn and Ben Buck, navigation is simple, the going underfoot is good and the views are excellent.

Start at the car park at Alva Glen, at the north end of Alva, and head into the glen, initially walking past a waterfall and then up a series of steps before having to walk under a water-supply pipe. Ten metres after the pipe turn right and walk past a small, fenced-in building (chlorine store) to arrive at a metal-sprung gate. Pass through the gate onto open ground and follow the path uphill to the vehicle track, buffeted by gorse bushes along the way.

Continue along the vehicle track as it rises and doubles back on itself a couple of times. Just as the track straightens to run parallel with Silver Burn on the right, take the vehicle track on the left and stay on this track as it contours around the Nebit and above Alva Glen until the burn is crossed on concrete slabs at GR884987.

After crossing the burn continue for approximately 30–50m and turn right to ascend without a clear path (but over easy ground) up the grassy flank of the Craighorn ridge, also known as the Ogles. Ascend steadily for a distance of approximately 700m before the ground levels out at the start of the ridge.

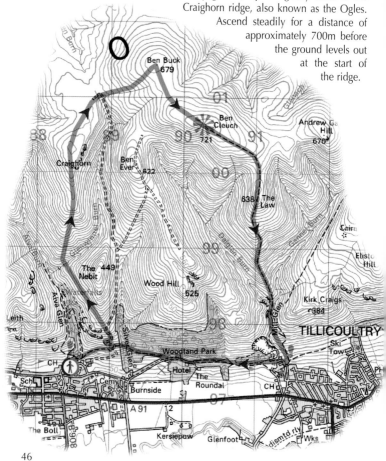

Alva Glen from the slopes of Craighorn

▸ Continue directly north from this point on a vague path, but essentially just maintaining a course along the centre of the ridge, gaining height gradually over the distance of 800m to the summit of Craighorn (583m), marked by a wooden stake in a small collection of stones.

Leaving Craighorn in a rough northeasterly direction the path becomes indistinct, but the aim is to make for the start of the vehicle track at the head of the Glenwinnel Burn (GR888010). A bearing should be taken from the Craighorn summit to this point in low visibility. Approximately 30m from the start of the wide vehicle track (and just where the track bends), turn left on a distinguishable grassy path and ascend fairly gradually uphill on this path to reach the summit of Ben Buck (679m) after a distance of just under 1km. Views from here are limited to those to the north, as the large spine of Ben Cleuch obscures views south and demonstrates the lack of separation from other peaks that means despite its height Ben Buck fails to achieve Donald status.

From here is an excellent view of the pronounced form of the Nebit to the south and to the west the impressively steep, east-facing slopes of the Bengengie ridge.

47

From Ben Buck follow the faint path in a southerly direction, running parallel to the fence to reach another fence, at which point cross over the stile and turn left uphill for a distance of 400m to arrive at the summit of Ben Cleuch (721m), the highest point in the Ochils range.

> From the summit of Ben Cleuch is a 360 degree panorama: in the northwest the Crianlarich Hills and the distinctive peaks of the Lawers range above the Strathearn Valley; westward the ever-present Ben Lomond and Ben Ledi; stretching south, the fertile plains of the Forth and Devon valleys parallel the line of the Ochils range, eventually meeting the isolated Lomond Hills in the east.

Leave the summit following the path in a southeasterly direction, still staying parallel to the fence. The obvious path bends around to join the short ridge and then summit of the Law, marked by a small cairn on the other side of the fence. From this point the descent directly south in Mill Glen starts, moving over good ground that is steep in parts, and can occasionally be muddy and slippery on the well-used paths. The descent becomes steepest just before reaching the convergence of the Daiglen and Gannel Burns, and a short scramble down leads to a small footbridge over the Gannel Burn. Just after the footbridge ascend to the maintained path over rocky and often slippery ground to then descend on the maintained path into Mill Glen.

Once out of the glen, cross the burn and walk along the streets past the Clock Mill to the second turning right into Scotland Place. Head to the tarmac at the end of the road and turn right onto the path that moves for a few metres through undergrowth.

On reaching the next road turn right again, and after a few more metres take the gravel path marked by the wooden sign indicating 'Alva 3km'. Continuing along this path on open ground with the golf course on the left, Wood Hill Wood is soon entered. A fine old building called 'The Stables' is passed, and soon after the path rejoins the car park.

To return to the car park via the lower slopes of the Nebit, head along the diagonal path almost immediately opposite the car park and enter the woodland, following the path as it rises westerly under the shady sycamore canopy. After almost 500m, as a smaller path joins from the right, continue westwards to cross Silver Burn, with the fenced-off remains of an old mine shaft just to the left. Pass through the gate at the end of the woods onto the lower slopes of the Nebit.

Descend the vehicle track used at the start of the walk and take the footpath, also used on the ascent, to find the way back to Alva Glen and the start of the walk.

Early morning mist seen from the summit of Ben Cleuch

WALK 6
The Nebit

Distance	4km
Height gain	409m
Time	1hr 30min
Difficulty rating	2
Maps required	OS Landranger 58 (1:50,000)
	OS Explorer 366 (1:25,000)
	Harvey's Map – Ochil Hills (1:25,000)
Start point	car park for Alva Glen (GR885975)

A short yet highly satisfying and uncomplicated circular walk up one of the more distinctively shaped hills in the Ochils. Almost entirely encircled by watercourses, the Nebit is clearly separate from the larger peaks around it, and with the exception of Dumyat is perhaps the most defined peak in the range.

The route initially takes the maintained path following Alva Glen, rising above dramatic gorge cliffs and including the popular viewpoint at Smuggler's Cave. Continuing along the glen, crossing the burn near an impressive waterfall, the route moves over undefined but easy ground to the summit, before descending south and circling back to Alva Glen.

From Alva Glen car park, at the north end of Alva, follow the path into the glen alongside Alva Burn. Popular year round, the glen is completely fenced in to allow for the natural regeneration of its hazel, ash and rowan trees.

The glen lacks the immediate sense of wilderness that the other Ochils glens have, partly because of the manmade dams and lakes that were originally built to maintain the flow of water to the Alva mills, but also because of the fences next to the path that are necessary to protect against some enormous drops. However, the upper sections of the glen, where huge gorge walls fall sharply to the burn below, are perhaps the most breathtaking in the region, with Smuggler's Cave a justifiably popular viewpoint at the upper glen. Birdlife is abundant, with grey wagtails particularly noticeable in most of the lower wooded section, and kestrels often seen on the grassy slopes of the Nebit and Wee Torry.

Shortly after passing the first dam, the path ascends on concrete steps under a large water-supply pipe, then heads left and through a sprung-metal gate now high above the burn. After passing Alva Dam the path ascends more steeply, and narrows to a series of switchback tracks that quickly gain height before levelling out and arriving at the viewpoint for Smuggler's Cave. From here, cross at the stile and descend right (the left-hand route provides a pleasant contour around the slopes of Wee Torry and will return to the car park).

A diversion can be taken downhill to the cave, but the route continues along the glen for approximately 400m to the Spout of Craighorn, where the Glenwinnel Burn meets Alva Burn. Pass over the small outcrop that overlooks the meeting of the burns and descend to cross the burn upstream of the burns' convergence. Once on the eastern side of the Alva Burn, head back downstream to cross the narrower Glenwinnel Burn just below an impressive waterfall.

Head up the moderately steep incline of the Nebit's northwestern spur, gradually moving away from the waterfall, and on reaching the farm track, go through the gate and follow the fenceline upwards for approximately 30m, before turning towards slightly rougher ground and rocks in a southeasterly direction to reach the unmarked but obvious summit of the hill (449m).

Waterfall of the Glenwinnel Burn

The Nebit proves to be an excellent vantage point, both for views out to the Forth Valley and to the larger surrounding hills in which it nestles. To the west, the long line and peak of the Bengengie ridge, with the unusual gully between Torry and Wee Torry; directly north the southern flanks of the Craighorn ridge, known as the Ogles, and to the east the Ben Ever ridge, Silver Burn and Wood Hill Wood.

From the top, descend south along the grassy path that dissects the summit onto the south face of the Nebit, known as 'the Gowls'. On reaching the farm track, follow it as it moves east towards Silver Burn, and join the main farm track as it zigzags downwards. On the second bend, however, about 5m before the large metal gate, strike right and southwesterly off the track onto a vague grassy path. With the large Stroud Mill building now in view, the path descends gradually until it reaches another metal-sprung gate and the return entrance to Alva Glen.

WALK 7
Wood Hill

Distance	5.6km
Height gain	505m
Time	1hr 50min
Difficulty rating	2
Maps required	OS Landranger 58 (1:50,000)
	OS Explorer 366 (1:25,000)
	Harvey's Map – Ochil Hills (1:25,000)
Start point	car park, Wood Hill (GR899975)

A very enjoyable circular walk that despite being short is in no way lacking in variety or interest, combining a mixture of woodland walking, excellent summit views and a descent into the popular Mill Glen.

Beginning in perhaps the best section of woodland in the Ochils – Wood Hill Wood – a defined path rises quickly through different levels of forestry. The initial shaded sycamore canopy opens up to mixed woodland of oak and beech, which then leads to a crown of ancient Scots pines at the top of the wood.

Basic macronavigation is required to follow natural features for a short period from the summit before rejoining well-established paths above Mill Glen.

Ample parking is available at the car park at the foot of Wood Hill, situated off the A91 between Alva and Tillicoultry. From the car park entrance head almost directly across to the diagonal path and immediately enter the woodland, following the path as it rises westerly under the shady sycamore canopy. After almost 500m, as a smaller path joins from the right, continue westwards before reaching Silver Burn.

Approximately one metre before reaching the slatted wooden crossing point at the burn, head right off the

53

main path on an easily missed path, and after half a metre turn right again into an even less obvious path that is initially hidden by gorse bushes. Once through the gorse the path is unmistakable, and climbs quite steeply through open mixed woodland, passing a small crooked oak tree and then a small slabby outcrop before turning at a right angle to head northeasterly, continuing to ascend to a fence, with a sign 'Rhodders Farm'.

Carefully cross this fence and continue on the path up to the fine collection of Scots pines that dominate the skyline, slightly reminiscent of the larger tracts of the Caledonian forest further north in Scotland. The path reaches the edge of these trees and ascends by the side of them with fine views of the Nebit and Wee Torry to the west. ◀

> At this point it is worth taking the time to explore this area of high woodland before returning to the path.

The path continues more gradually upwards, over good ground. After approximately 500m it appears to peter out at what seems to be a small drainage ditch with rocks lining one side. Follow this ditch and the now vague path until it reaches an area with rocky scree deposits, the ditch becoming wider and slightly deeper. At this point, leaving any paths, ascend the bank, aiming towards the highest point, which eventually leads to the summit of Wood Hill (525m), marked by a small cairn.

Head 200m in a northeasterly direction from the summit to reach the distinctive gully that precedes the start of Wood Burn (a bearing will be necessary in poor conditions). Walking along the bottom of this initially rocky depression the start of the burn is quickly reached. Continue to follow the burn, crossing

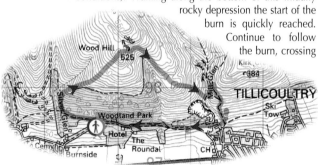

The serene Wood Hill Wood

the fence that intersects it before reaching a second fence at the corner of the Scots pines. Do not attempt to cross this fence – instead, head southeasterly, ascending over a small tussocky bank, and continue in this direction for approximately 300m to reach another shallow gully and what appears to be an old, rock-strewn track marked by a narrow band of visible earth, possibly from subsidence.

Stay on this track, with the bulk of the Law now directly ahead, until it reaches the main path that runs parallel and above the side of Mill Glen. Turn right here and walk above Mill Glen, reaching a conical-shaped cairn, at which point a less-defined path that descends left needs to be taken. This path reaches the fence and the warning sign at the edge of the quarry before switching direction and descending back in the direction of the Law. ◄ Head towards the bridge and exit the glen via the main path.

Please note that care should be taken at this point. There are some sheer drops into Mill Glen that are unfenced and deceptively covered with shrubbery.

Once out of the glen, cross the burn and go past the Clock Mill. Turning right into Scotland Place, head to the tarmac at the end of the road and turn right onto the path that moves for a few metres through undergrowth. On reaching the next road turn right again, and after a few more metres take the gravel path marked by the wooden sign indicating 'Alva 3km'. Continuing along this path on open ground with the golf course on the left, Wood Hill Wood is soon re-entered. A fine old building called 'The Stables' is passed, and soon after the path rejoins the car park.

Wood Hill

WALK 8
Ben Cleuch Circuit

Distance	A) 10.2km, B) 9km
Height gain	671m
Time	A) 3hr 30min, B) 3hr
Difficulty rating	3
Maps required	OS Landranger 58 (1:50,000)
	OS Explorer 366 (1:25,000)
	Harvey's Map – Ochil Hills (1:25,000)
Start point	Mill Glen in Tillicoultry (GR914975)

Despite being the highest peak in the Ochils (721m), Ben Cleuch lies reclusively out of sight from the foot of its southern escarpment. Hidden by the steep slopes of the Law and the Ben Ever ridge, the energetic start this route requires is soon rewarded as height and views are gained quickly.

Once on the horseshoe ridge, well-defined paths and boundary lines make for simple navigation, allowing you time to enjoy some of the best views in the Ochils.

From Ben Ever there is the choice of descending into Silver Glen and returning through the charming woodland walk of Wood Hill Wood, route **A)**, or alternatively continuing along the fine Ben Ever ridge back to Mill Glen, route **B)**. For a more gradual ascent the route can be walked in a clockwise direction, although descent from the Law in wet weather can be equally challenging.

Parking is available at the bottom of Mill Glen, adjacent to the Clock Mill and at the top of Upper Mill Street, sign-posted from the main road.

Follow the well-maintained path through the glen, with the burn initially on the left-hand side, passing several interesting features along the way. The first of these is a small gully that passes underneath a cave

57

known locally as 'the Lion's Den'. This gully indicates the actual line of the Ochil Fault, the crack in the Earth's crust that formed the Ochils. Soon after, the open-cast remains of the Alva Quarry are visible to the left. ◄

With a keen eye fixed on the fast-flowing burn there is often the chance to spot a variety of birdlife, including dippers and grey wagtails, as well as small mammals such as mink and voles.

Continue along the path, switching back and forth across a series of bridges for 10 minutes before sheer gorge walls open up into gorse- and grass-covered hillside. Ignore any rough paths diverting onto the hillside until the head of the glen is reached at the convergence of the Daiglen and Gannel Burns. With the bottom of the Law now in view, leave the maintained path as it switches back in a hairpin and descend towards the wooden slatted bridge visible over the Gannel Burn. Care should be taken on this short descent, as there are often greasy rocks underfoot. This area is popular year round, and can become quite congested on fine summer days.

Starting the steep walk up The Law © Joe Buchanan

Immediately after crossing the Gannel Burn a small scramble brings you to the defined path at the foot of the Law. What follows is a demanding ascent up the steep slopes of the Law, but spectacular views and speedy height gain are more than compensation for aching calf muscles. In approximately 55 minutes the summit of the Law is reached, marked by a small cairn on the other side of the boundary fence. ▶

Head directly north from the Law, keeping left of the fenceline. The path initially runs parallel to the fence, often over quite boggy ground, but bends around in a gradually northwesterly direction to the broad summit of Ben Cleuch. In poor visibility the fence can act as a useful navigational aid, as it runs directly from the summit of the Law to meet another fence at 90 degrees, which if then followed northwesterly will lead directly to the surprisingly rock-strewn and cluttered summit of Ben Cleuch.

The benefit of climbing to the highest peak in the region is the unchallenged panoramic views afforded from its summit, perhaps the best in central Scotland. To the

From here an impressive range of fellow Ochil summits can be viewed. To the east, King's Seat and Tarmangie Hill; directly north the whaleback summits of Andrew Gannel Hill and Ben Cleuch, and to the west the impressively steep eastern flank of the Ben Ever ridge.

Looking down The Law

northeast the Cairngorm Massif; in the northwest the Crainlarich Hills and the distinctive peaks of the Lawers range above the Strathearn Valley; westward the everpresent Ben Lomond and Ben Ledi; stretching south, the carseland of the Forth and Devon valleys parallels the line of the Ochils, eventually meeting the isolated Lomond Hills in the east.

Follow the obvious grassy track from the summit as it initially continues northwesterly, but gradually descends southwesterly to the col before the Ben Ever ridge. At the intersection of the three fences, cross at the stile and gradually ascend along the southerly path for 500m to the barely distinguishable summit of Ben Ever (622m), marked only by a few cairn stones. Descend southeasterly along the ridge for 300m until the path splits just before a small, boggy pool. The left-hand fork offers alternative route B) (below) as it continues along the Ben Ever ridge, returning to the start point via Mill Glen.

A) Wood Hill Wood

To follow route **A)**, take the right-hand fork and enjoy the gentle grassy descent towards Silver Glen and the bulbous mass of the Nebit, until a farm track and some sheep pens are reached. Turn left and continue along the farm track, passing a densely wooded plantation, staying on the track through a series of loops until a sign marked 'Public Footpath', by the edge of the natural woodland, indicates the entrance to Wood Hill Wood. Once in the wood, lower or upper paths may be taken.

After 1.3km the path exits the wood into open ground by the golf course, and then reaches a tarmac road from where a right turn should be taken, shortly followed by cutting through the shrubs on the left-hand side and continuing onto the estate at Scotland Street, after which Upper Mill Street is arrived at just down from the Clock Mill and the car park.

B) Mill Glen

From the small, boggy pool reached just after descending from the summit of Ben Ever, take the left-hand route where the path forks, continuing along the ridge over good ground and descending slightly for 200m. The path is obvious, although it begins to taper somewhat as it starts to ascend again from the mid-point on the ridge.

The path runs parallel to and then crosses a fence. Soon after crossing the fence the descent from the ridge begins. Now quite faint, the path descends in a south-easterly direction along the main spur on the other side of Wood Hill until the ground evens out, reaching what appears to be an old, rock-strewn track marked by a narrow band of visible earth, possibly from subsidence.

Stay on this track, with the bulk of the Law now directly ahead, until it reaches the main path that runs along the side of Mill Glen. Turn right here and walk above Mill Glen, reaching a conical-shaped cairn, at which point a less-defined path that descends left needs to be taken. This path reaches the fence and the warning sign at the edge of the quarry before switching direction and descending back in the direction of the Law. **Please note** that care should be taken at this point. There are some sheer drops into Mill Glen that are unfenced and deceptively covered with shrubbery.

Continue on the path and cross the high metal bridge to descend back into Mill Glen and return to the start of the walk.

WALK 9
Mill Glen to Dollar Glen

Distance	8.2km
Height gain	648m
Time	2hr 40min
Difficulty rating	2
Maps required	OS Landranger 58 (1:50,000)
	OS Explorer 366 (1:25,000)
	Harvey's Map – Ochil Hills (1:25,000)
Start point	public car park at Mill Glen, Tillicoultry (GR914975)

Linking the towns of Tillicoultry and Dollar, this point-to-point walk connects two picturesque Ochil glens via the high ground of King's Seat. This relatively undemanding route gains height gradually, following the well-established path northeasterly above Andrew Gannel Burn, before turning onto the broad summit of King's Seat and descending the popular path to Castle Campbell and Dollar Glen.

This route also provides the basis for combining countless other walks, either as a start point into the Ochils range, or as an exit back to the Hillfoots.

Car parking is available at either end of the walk, or alternatively a regular bus service runs between the two towns to provide an easy return to the start point.

Instead of heading into the glen, follow the sign marked 'Public Path' that leads east from the car park and take the steps marked by the yellow arrow of the Ranger Service. At the top of the steps, go through the metal-sprung gate onto open ground amongst gorse bushes.

Follow the obvious path as it leads uphill, with the unavoidable sight of the open quarry to the left. When the path forks, avoid the lower (left-hand) path that descends into Mill Glen, instead staying on the higher

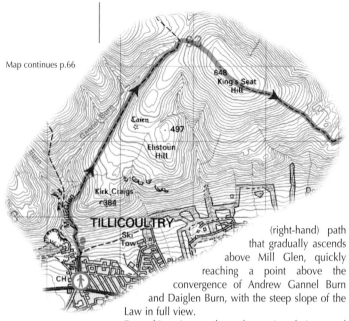

Map continues p.66

(right-hand) path that gradually ascends above Mill Glen, quickly reaching a point above the convergence of Andrew Gannel Burn and Daiglen Burn, with the steep slope of the Law in full view.

From this point on, the path remains obvious, and occasionally boggy in parts, as it climbs very gradually in a northeasterly direction above the channel carved by the Gannel Burn. Remain on this path for almost 2.5km, passing three major burns that are useful indicators of location, until eventually reaching the obvious col at the head of the burn. From the col, carefully cross the fence and ascend southeasterly, without an obvious path, up the broad northwestern flank of King's Seat, reaching the unassuming summit of the hill, marked by a few small stones.

Continue easterly for 250m to reach the cairn stone shelter, often mistaken for King's Seat summit, and descend the defined path, passing a series of linear gullies (the Banks of Dollar) before reaching boggy ground at the broad col. Passing through the gate, continue along the path in the direction of Bank Hill, and

Burn in spate flowing into the Gannel Burn

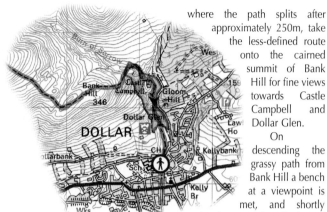

where the path splits after approximately 250m, take the less-defined route onto the cairned summit of Bank Hill for fine views towards Castle Campbell and Dollar Glen.

On descending the grassy path from Bank Hill a bench at a viewpoint is met, and shortly after a gate into the fenced area of the glen. Once through the gate in front of the sign warning of the dangerous cliff edge, there are two route options, both leading to Castle Campbell. The right-hand path heads down Jacob's Ladder – a series of switchback steps – but stay on the left-hand path and cross the bridge by a pleasant waterfall and pool. ◀ The path continues to descend into an almost rainforest environment, with damp mosses and ferns clinging to the rocks above the huge, plunging cliffs of the Sauchie Falls, one of the most impressive sights in the Ochils.

Care must be taken here, as although the path is predominantly fenced there are still sections without fences and some large drops.

The path arrives in front of Castle Campbell, with the route to the top car park found by following the tarmac road round to the left for another couple of minutes.

For accessing public transport back to the start point, descend the maintained paths into the glen to the north of Dollar and continue through the town for five minutes before reaching the A91, the main road that goes through Dollar, from where buses can be caught.

WALK 10
Castle Campbell Circuit

Distance	10.3km
Height gain	760m
Time	3hr 20min
Difficulty rating	3
Maps required	OS Landranger 58 (1:50,000)
	OS Explorer 366 (1:25,000)
	Harvey's Map – Ochil Hills (1:25,000)
Start point	Hillfoots car park, Dollar (GR965985)

An impressive ridge walk that starts in the precipitous woodland confines of Dollar Glen, but rises to over 640m, and includes three of the eight Donalds in the Ochils: King's Seat, Tarmangie Hill and Whitewisp Hill. From the grassy whaleback ridges of this circular walk, constantly shifting panoramas combine to provide some of the best views in central Scotland.

Easily accessible from the town of Dollar, the walk is relatively undemanding, over good ground, but with some requirement for basic navigational skills in bad weather. In more testing conditions there is also the option of returning from the halfway point of the walk through the more sheltered Glen of Sorrow.

Three car parks provide access to Castle Campbell and the hills, but it is worthwhile beginning at the bottom car park (marked Hillfoots car park) just above Dollar museum to include the pleasant woodland walk through Dollar Glen.

From the car park turn left and then immediately right. As the road continues upwards take the left track descending into Dollar Glen. Cross Dollar Burn at the wooden bridge and then ascend through a series of steps and the switchback path to the edge of the treeline by the

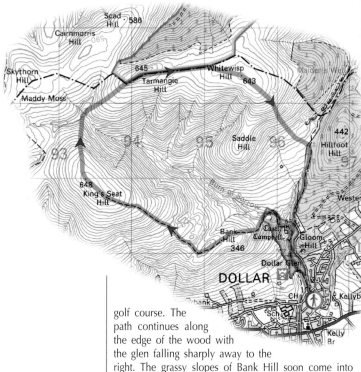

golf course. The
path continues along
the edge of the wood with
the glen falling sharply away to the
right. The grassy slopes of Bank Hill soon come into
view, as does an impressive first sighting of Castle
Campbell from a gap in the treeline. Ahead, as the path
reaches a fence the option of descending towards the
castle must be ignored. Instead, cross the stile to the left
onto open ground and ascend the shoulder of Bank Hill.
A small cairn marks the top of Bank Hill.

From Bank Hill follow the vague southwesterly path
for 300m, skirting some small knolls, until reaching the
gate at the broad col. Once past the col the path switches
to a northwesterly direction, picking its way through a
series of small linear gullies, known locally as the Banks
of Dollar, until the straightforward route to the top of
King's Seat comes into view. The path takes in a series of

terraced knolls (which to the uninitiated each falsely promise the summit), until the slope does eventually open to the summit plateau of King's Seat. A cairn and some shelter stones are immediately obvious. However, for the purposes of Donald-bagging and taking bearings, the actual summit is a barely distinguishable point marked by a smaller collection of cairn stones 250m northwest along the ridge.

From this point bear north, descending the main spur steeply towards the junction of two burns, marking the head of the Glen of Sorrow and the halfway point of the walk. A clearly defined path from the head of the glen follows the Burn of Sorrow for 3km, providing a sheltered return to Castle Campbell in poor weather.

To continue the ridge walk, cross the first burn above the rockpool where the two burns meet, heading upstream 10–15m for the best place to cross the second burn. Ascend the shoulder of Tarmangie Hill without a visible path for a distance of 200m until the ground evens out to reveal the distinct main ridge, split in half by the drystone dyke and fenceposts of the boundary line. Cross the boundary fence to meet the ridge path again and follow it towards the cairn at Tarmangie Hill.

Castle Campbell and Dollar Glen

Once at Tarmangie summit the contrasting northern panorama is evident; the bulk of the Caingorms loom ominously in the far north, with the peaks of Ben Vorlich, Stuc a Chroin, Ben More and the Lawers range easy to identify in the near distance. The true moorland character of the interior Ochils also unfolds from this point, tapering down towards the fertile flood plains of Strathearn.

The route leaves the cairn at Tarmangie and follows a faint grassy path, first crossing and then moving away from the boundary fence for a distance of just over 1km, reaching the obvious summit cairn of Whitewisp Hill without losing or gaining much height. Descent from Whitewisp follows the shoulder of the hill in a south-easterly direction for a further 1km before meeting the track at the edge of Hillfoot Hill forest. Due to the very broad summit of Whitewisp, it is advisable to take a bearing from here in conditions of poor visibility.

Follow the Hillfoot track for 1.5km, arriving back at the car park for Castle Campbell. Turn right and descend towards the castle. Take the left-hand footpath 10m before the castle entrance and descend steeply into the spectacular ravine left of the castle. Cross the burn at the bridge and follow the path directly to the bottom of Dollar Glen to rejoin the start of the walk.

WALK 11
Tillicoultry to Blackford

Distance	14.2km
Height gain	580m
Time	3hr 50min
Difficulty rating	4
Maps required	OS Landranger 58 (1:50,000)
	OS Explorer 366 (1:25,000)
	Harvey's Map – Ochil Hills (1:25,000)
Start point	car park, Mill Glen, Tillicoultry (GR914975)

This long, point-to-point walk retraces the old drovers' route across the Ochils between the two towns of Tillicoultry and Blackford, where it is possible to leave vehicles at either end of the route. Heading south to north, the majority of the height gain is achieved in the first three kilometres of walking, thus allowing a gentle descent towards Blackford, but the route can also easily be made in the opposite direction.

Although this route is marked both on the map and signposted as a public footpath, there are significant sections where no path is actually visible on the ground. Navigation and terrain at times can therefore be challenging.

Start at the public car park at Mill Glen, Tillicoultry. Instead of heading into the glen, follow the sign marked 'Public Path' that leads east from the car park and take the steps marked by the yellow arrow of the Ranger Service. At the top of the steps, go through the metal-sprung gate into open ground amongst gorse bushes. Follow the obvious path as it leads uphill with the unavoidable sight of the open quarry to the left.

When the path forks, avoid the lower (left-hand) path that descends into Mill Glen, instead staying on the higher (right-hand) path that gradually ascends above

Mill Glen, quickly reaching a point above the convergence of the Gannel Burn and Daiglen Burn with the steep slope of the Law in full view.

From this point on the path remains obvious, and occasionally boggy in parts, as it climbs very gradually in a northeasterly direction above the channel carved by the Gannel Burn. Remain on this path for almost 2.5km, passing three major burns that are useful indicators of location, until eventually reaching the obvious col at the head of the Gannel Burn. Cross left over the boggy area of watershed, bending at almost 90 degrees to start to ascend the lower eastern flank of Andrew Gannel Hill.

The well-worn path soon deviates from the marked path on the map as it continues straight up the eastern spur of the hill towards the summit of Andrew Gannel Hill.

The path that is actually marked on the map is the less obvious path that branches off this main path approximately 200m after taking the right-angle turn. While this discrepancy between map and actual paths seems confusing, the required path simply runs parallel to the fence that heads northwesterly towards Maddy Moss, crossing a minor burn 400m before reaching a stile at the fence on the col between Andrew Gannel Hill and Skythorn Hill (the highest point of the walk).

Once over the fence the well-worn path initially runs next to the fence towards Skythorn Hill. This actual path is again slightly different to the

Map continues p.74

marked route on the map, which immediately contours around Skythorn. Head northeasterly for 100m from the col to then take the obvious left-hand path that moves along the Skythorn Ridge and above the Broich Burn in a northerly direction over some boggy ground in parts. ▸

The route descends to the col between the ridges of Skythorn and Frandy Moss, to pass through a gate at GR919025 and into some fairly soft ground, but the path is visible to the left of the gate and the ground improves swiftly as the path begins to rise again, maintaining a course contouring above Broich Glen. Almost 1km after passing through the gate at the col, a small but significant burn comes into view on the right, at which point the path peters out. The best route is to descend on the fairly steep grass slopes to cross the burn from the right at its lower, flattening level.

After crossing the burn continue in the direction of Upper Glendevon Reservoir and a vehicle track should soon be visible, as is a bridge crossing the Broich Burn. Cross this bridge and proceed up the vehicle track towards Backhills Farm for 100m to take the signposted public footpath to the right. This crosses a muddy field for 50m and then reaches a stile and a burn, both of which are crossed to continue running parallel to the southern arm of the reservoir.

Another stile is reached at GR910039. Cross the burn that follows the stile and clamber up the steep bank to enter onto open ground once more. From this point the path that is marked on the map in actual fact disappears on the ground, but its general route should be followed as it heads northwards towards a small patch of coniferous forestry before crossing the burn at GR909042.

Still without an actual path, stay with the presumed path on the map, which essentially skirts the southern edge of the reservoir, passing over some challenging terrain, including several peat hags, to reach a small fenced inlet at GR903044, before proceeding to the western end of the reservoir. Frustratingly, the nearest crossing point to the other side of the reservoir is the bridge over the River Devon feeding into the reservoir

Looking back from this ridge the impressive bulk of Ben Cleuch and Ben Buck is seen, as well as fine views of the picturesque and remote glens of the Glenach Burn and the Grodwell Burn.

from the west. Fortunately, though, as the route moves alongside the Devon the path becomes evident on the ground once more and the bridge across the Devon is easy to spot.

Once over the bridge, head back in the opposite direction on improving ground to arrive back at the edge of the reservoir near the ruins of a building which is marked on the map. Continue past the ruined building, on a now obvious path, towards Glen Bee, and cross the ladder over the drystone dyke and then the burn to rejoin the path, which moves uphill slightly along Glen Bee to reach a vehicle track approximately 600m from the reservoir. At the vehicle track the going underfoot instantly improves and route finding once again becomes simple.

Stay with the track as it heads in a vaguely northwesterly direction, reaching a wide wooden gate after approximately 400m. The gate enters onto a more established track at a hairpin bend, where the lower left-hand section of the track should be taken, continuing along the Glen of Kinpauch and eventually bending around past a forestry plantation in amongst heather moorland. The track eventually reaches a right-angle turn at GR896071. It continues for 400m, passing near, but not visibly past, Kinpauch Farm, to turn at a right angle again and pass by another small plantation on the right-hand side.

Just after the plantation the track bends sharply again and proceeds straight ahead towards Blackford for approximately 800m, to reach a fence that leads out onto a minor road next to the A9, which is the best place to leave any return vehicles.

WALK 12
Innerdownie Ridge

Distance	13.1km
Height gain	558m
Time	3hr 30min
Difficulty rating	3
Maps required	OS Landranger 58 (1:50,000)
	OS Explorer 366 (1:25,000)
	Harvey's Map – Ochil Hills (1:25,000)
Start point	Castle Campbell car park, Dollar (GR963993)

A straightforward and popular circular walk, linking the town of Dollar to the village of Glendevon, over the longest defined ridge in the Ochils. The first half of the route moves over high ground, and includes the two Donald peaks of Whitewisp Hill and Innerdownie, before descending to Glendevon, with the opportunity for pub refreshment at the halfway point. The second half of the route returns along a level path next to the Glenquey Reservoir. Apart from the first section of the walk to the summit of Saddle Hill, well-used paths exist for the majority of the route, making navigation simple and conditions underfoot generally favourable.

Descend from the car park towards the castle, crossing the Burn of Care. Approximately 50m after the burn and 30m before the entrance to the castle, turn right up onto the steep bank, where an indistinct path should be just about visible.

King's Seat and Saddle Hill soon come into view as the bank levels out with Castle Campbell below. From this point all paths lead off to Bank Hill, and there is no direct path to Saddle Hill, so a route must be taken straight across the gradually sloping and in parts slightly boggy ground in a northwesterly direction to the base of the hill.

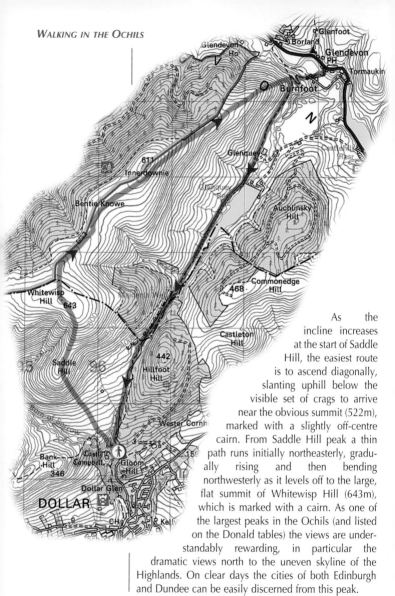

As the incline increases at the start of Saddle Hill, the easiest route is to ascend diagonally, slanting uphill below the visible set of crags to arrive near the obvious summit (522m), marked with a slightly off-centre cairn. From Saddle Hill peak a thin path runs initially northeasterly, gradually rising and then bending northwesterly as it levels off to the large, flat summit of Whitewisp Hill (643m), which is marked with a cairn. As one of the largest peaks in the Ochils (and listed on the Donald tables) the views are understandably rewarding, in particular the dramatic views north to the uneven skyline of the Highlands. On clear days the cities of both Edinburgh and Dundee can be easily discerned from this peak.

Looking across to Bank Hill from Saddle Hill

As numerous paths meet at the cairn, leave Whitewisp summit following the thin, roughly north-westerly path (compass work maybe required here in poor weather), and after approximately 250m, where three fences intersect, a substantial deer-fence is met with a large ladder (the east side of the ridge is an enclosed area managed by the Woodland Trust). Cross over this ladder and continue along the obvious grassy track with the fence on the left-hand side.

Attention is required 150–200m after crossing the ladder, as at least two large bogs half covered in vegetation lie across the route of the path. These bogs are easily missed and in wet conditions are potentially very dangerous. After easily navigating these hazards the ridge walk is pleasant and solid underfoot, with the summit of Innerdownie (611m) reached without any further difficulties. ▸

The obvious path continues from the summit of Innerdownie, descending gradually for approximately 2km to reach Glenquey Hill, at which point the pretty village of Glendevon comes into view. Nestling in amongst rolling hills and forestry, with the River Devon looping through it, Glendevon appears in an almost picture-postcard setting. Descend until a grassy farm track is met as it contours around the base of Glenquey Hill. Cross over the farm track and continue down, as

The summit (another Donald) is marked by a cairn, but more usefully, 15m before the actual summit an excellent stone-built snug is propped against a large rocky slab, providing much-needed protection in bad conditions, and this is often a preferable place to stop instead of the summit.

indicated by the waymarking sign with the yellow arrow, passing through a large gate in the deer-fence to meet a tarmac road at Burnfoot by several houses, which leads to a small stone bridge.

Immediately after crossing the stone bridge, turn left through the wooden gate by the sign that points towards Glendevon and continue along the open field to reach the metal footbridge, which is crossed to arrive at the main road through Glendevon. Turn right and after 100m is the welcome sight of the Tormaukin Inn.

After rest and refreshment at the inn, retrace the path back to the waymarking sign with the yellow arrow at the base of Glenquey Hill. At this point turn left onto the easy, almost level track that reaches the dam end of Glenquey Reservoir after 1.5km, after which the path turns into a more maintained vehicle track all the way to the southern end of the reservoir. As the track ends, continue in the same direction on the well-trodden path, crossing a stile and then a small burn with some marshy ground to the left, before arriving at a series of knolls with the northern corner of the Hillfoot Hill forest plantation on the left.

Ignore any options to follow the path into the forest, and after approximately 1.5km walking on this path, just as King's Seat and Bank Hill come into view, join the farm track that leads down to the white cottage and the car park at Castle Campbell.

Evening view above the pretty village of Glendevon

WALK 13
Kirk Burn Glen Circuit

Distance	3.8km
Height gain	370m
Time	1hr 20min
Difficulty rating	2
Maps required	OS Landranger 58 (1:50,000)
	OS Explorer 366 (1:25,000)
	Harvey's Map – Ochil Hills (1:25,000)
Start point	west of Tillicoultry (GR926974)

The Kirk Burn Glen is a small, well-formed and generally quiet alternative to the larger and busier glens on the southern escarpment of the Ochils. A fast-flowing burn and steep crags, combined with close proximity to the east of Tillicoultry, mean that this walk is not only interesting but also particularly accessible. Route finding and terrain are relatively easy, but some movement on fairly steep ground, in particular on the descent, is required.

From the A91, west of Tillicoultry, turn left into Bard's Way, a cul-de-sac that gives access to a modern housing development on the eastern edge of Tillicoultry. Drive up Bard's Way until a T-junction is reached at the top of the cul-de-sac, turn left and drive less than 50m to where the road ends. Unrestricted parking is available here.

A track is visible 20m directly ahead from the parking spot. Turn right on reaching this broad track and begin to head uphill in the direction of Kirk Burn Glen for approximately 250m, with open fields on the right and a small copse on the left, arriving close to the fenced area marked as Kirkhill Reservoir.

Twenty metres before reaching the reservoir take the vehicle track that joins to the left by the large beech tree.

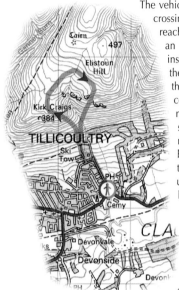

The vehicle track bends into the copse, soon crossing Kirk Burn to almost immediately reach a wooden farm gate that leads into an open field. At the gate turn right, instead of entering the field, and take the obvious path that heads uphill, through the predominantly silver birch copse, to reach a fence after approximately 150m. Cross over the fence to stand beside the burn in an area of mixed open land – gorse and bracken. Continue on the narrowing track as it picks its way quite steeply uphill through the gorse and bracken, running roughly parallel to the burn.

Once above the area of gorse a good view opens out into the small and pretty glen, with steep Easter Kirk Craig and its scree slope visible to the right, and a small waterfall at the steepest part of the burn directly in view ahead. To the left here a small ridge begins to rise, and there is the option to ascend the middle of this ridge in between some minor crags to reach the flat section above. However, to continue further into the glen, stay in between the ridge and the burn on the levelled patch of ground that climbs gradually left away from the burn and the waterfall to reach the flat ground just below the unmarked peak of 414m.

From this knoll great views of the larger Ochil peaks span west, including the Law and Andrew Gannel Hill, although Ben Cleuch is conspicuously tucked out of view from this point.

Cross over the obvious ruined dyke and head onto the small knoll of peak 414m. ◀ Head in a north-easterly direction from the knoll to the point where a fence crosses the top of Kirk Burn at GR923989 (a bearing may be necessary in poor weather, but in normal visibility the fenceposts should be visible). Before reaching the fence the going underfoot becomes slightly more difficult, as the grass becomes more tussocked, with damp areas to be avoided where possible.

Cross the narrow burn by the fence and head in a southeasterly direction, equivalent to the fence marked on the 1:25,000 map, although in reality at this point the fence ceases to exist for approximately 300m, after which its ramshackle posts can be spotted again and used as a simple navigational aid to reach its intersection with the drystone dyke (and fence) at GR926985.

At the intersection cross the fence and then the dyke and proceed right to where the dyke turns at a right angle and begin to descend. At this point there is a good sheltered spot to stop, with excellent views, on the left, just under a small set of crags.

The route off the hill here is initially fairly steep in parts, and despite being manageable, attention is still required to choose the easiest line of descent towards the dyke that borders Lady Ann's Wood. Once at the dyke turn right and head westwards to cross the dyke (that has descended from the hill), staying parallel and above the wood for 200m to arrive at Kirk Burn.

Cross the burn and the fence on the left, re-entering the silver birch copse and descending to the vehicle track that leads out to Kirkhill Reservoir and back to the start point.

Steep ground on the descent of the Kirk Glen route

WALK 14
Seamab Hill

Distance	7.5km
Height gain	194m
Time	1hr 50min
Difficulty rating	2
Maps required	OS Landranger 58 (1:50,000)
	OS Explorer 366 (1:25,000)
	Harvey's Map – Ochil Hills (1:25,000)
Start point	Castlehill Reservoir (GR997033)

Seamab Hill, the distinctive peak above Muckhart, is reached along the short ridge running west to east from the larger and broader Commonedge Hill, which itself is accessed on this walk by a gradual, slanting forest track. A fine southerly aspect to the ridge provides good views of a mesh of patchwork fields and trees below, particularly colourful in autumn. The route is circular, and although no distinct paths exist on the short ridge section, navigation and terrain are easy.

This area is often an excellent place to spot curlew. With their distinctive 'coor-lee' call and long curving beaks, curlew are quite unmistakable.

Parking is available at the large lay-by off the A823 next to the Castlehill Reservoir (GR997033). Cross the main road onto the Glenquey Reservoir access road, opposite, which slants gradually upwards into open ground. Continue on this road for approximately 1km, until shortly after the white cottage (Glenquey House) a track leads uphill on the left.

Ascend along this rougher track, gaining height as it switches back on itself twice before entering the forestry plantation. ◀ Immediately after entering the forestry area the track bends again sharply, after which the route stays on the track as it slants gradually upwards across Auchlinsky Hill for approximately 2km in a vague south-westerly direction. Ignore both opportunities to follow the track to the right, and continue to gradually ascend along the wide track until it peters out in open ground near the top of Commonedge Hill (396m).

Cross the fence that is now directly in view, then turning left but moving away from the fence, the spine of the ridge should soon be obvious. Despite the lack of any clear paths at this stage, the ground underfoot is good, and directionally the route simply heads towards the pronounced mass that is the peak of Seamab Hill at the end of the tapering ridge.

> The short ridge walk provides the best views of the route. Complex patterns of patchwork fields and hedgerows directly below present an untypical Scottish scene, perhaps more akin to the landscape of the Yorkshire Dales. Directly west, views of the Lomond Hills and Loch Leven come ever closer into view, and Castlehill Reservoir also makes an appearance from the mid-point of the ridge. It is not until the summit of Seamab, however, that these views culminate in an impressive panorama that on a clear day stretches as far as the North Sea.

Descend from the summit northeasterly, heading towards the drystone dyke at the corner of the forest plantation (GR995019). Cross over the dyke and walk gradually downhill next to it, crossing back over the fence to the left after 300m to access a small foot-bridge crossing the Auchlinsky Burn that is otherwise unseen (and unmarked on the map).

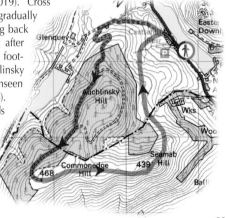

The footbridge leads directly onto a faint but increasingly visible quad track that ascends gradually on the other side of the burn and leads in a northerly direction to a sheepfold and a gate.

Walkers on the broad ridge to the summit of Seamab

Pass through the gate and stay on the track as it contours the side of the Auchlinsky Hill below the plantation, crossing a very small burn, after which point the track peters out somewhat. At this stage, however, the line of the initial access road should be evident, with several telegraph polls also indicating its presence. Head towards the access road and turn right on reaching it to shortly arrive back at the car park.

WALK 15
Frandy Burn Circuit

Distance	14.3km
Height gain	522m
Time	3hr 45min
Difficulty rating	3
Maps required	OS Landranger 58 (1:50,000)
	OS Explorer 366 (1:25,000)
	Harvey's Map – Ochil Hills (1:25,000)
Start point	lay-bys at Whitens (GR971053)

Beginning and ending in picturesque Glen Devon, this circular route moves through a working landscape of pasturelands, farms, commercial forestry and reservoirs. As such, it is an environment in constant change, with farm tracks and forestry appearing and disappearing faster than can be accurately mapped. Work on an extensive native woodland regeneration scheme by the Woodland Trust is particularly evident for the first half of the walk.

Following the hills that horseshoe Frandy Burn in the very heart of the Ochils, the circuit includes several peaks, most notably the knobbly summit of Ben Shee. While paths and farm tracks form a lot of the walk, they cannot always be relied upon for providing the correct direction, and do not necessarily offer the best of ground underfoot. Basic macronavigation, and in bad weather, compass bearings, will be necessary.

Heading towards Glen Eagles from Yetts o' Muckhart on the A823, parking is available in a couple of large lay-bys just after the forestry commission road at Whitens (GR971053).

Walk westwards along the main road for approximately 400m and turn up the private road marked for the Glensherup Fishery, crossing the attractive stone bridge and following the road around past the farm buildings. On reaching the fence after the farm buildings, cross right into open ground, and with no immediate path visible, ascend the shoulder of the ridge to meet a farm track which promptly arrives at a gate and stile. This fenceline marks a boundary for the Woodland Trust's native woodland regeneration scheme at Glensherup, which aims to regenerate 605 hectares of birch and oak woodland.

Cross at the stile, and instead of continuing on the farm track, move right onto a faint, grassy vehicle track that heads towards the broad top of the Shank (Harvey's Ochils 1:25,000 map). As a series of tracks criss-cross and scar the hill (evidence of the amount of work currently being undertaken in this section of the Ochils) stay on the middle of the ridge, heading southwesterly to the summit of Ben Shee (516m). ◀

From Ben Shee summit rejoin the wide and often boggy farm track that runs roughly along the centre of the ridge to Cairnmorris Hill. Stay on the track until it begins to contour around the ridge (approximately 200m after the small boggy pool at Mailer's Knowe), at which point leave the track and ascend over grassy tussocks to find an indistinct path on the top of Scad Hill (586m). This path continues to the unmarked summit of Cairnmorris Hill (606m) and then reaches the right angle at the boundary fence on the col before Skythorn Hill (601m).

The best all-round views of the walk are to be had from the summit of Ben Shee: Glen Eagles to the northwest; the pimpled summit of Innerdownie to the southwest; fine views along the ridge and the hills wrapped around the Frandy Burn

Grodwell Hill
553

At this point cross the stile and follow the boundary fence towards the flat summit of Skythorn, marked by a small cairn. From this point head northwesterly for approximately 150m to join the old drovers' path that leads from Mill Glen through to Glendevon Reservoir (a bearing maybe required at this point). Remain on this wide grassy path, heading northwards away from views of King's Seat and Ben Cleuch, to reach the fenceline at the watershed of the Frandy Burn – the halfway point of the walk.

Cross the stile at the fence and continue on the path northwards for 500m until the ground becomes less solid underfoot, the path petering out amongst large tussocks. Change direction at this point

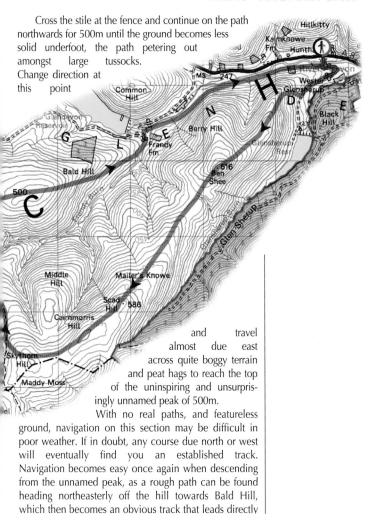

and travel almost due east across quite boggy terrain and peat hags to reach the top of the uninspiring and unsurprisingly unnamed peak of 500m.

With no real paths, and featureless ground, navigation on this section may be difficult in poor weather. If in doubt, any course due north or west will eventually find you an established track. Navigation becomes easy once again when descending from the unnamed peak, as a rough path can be found heading northeasterly off the hill towards Bald Hill, which then becomes an obvious track that leads directly to Frandy Farm.

On reaching the farm, go through the gates to bypass any of the sheep pens, and find the tarmac road after

Fence crossing on the way to Ben Shee

passing a small copse of Scots pine and a farmhouse. Exit down the slope at the first loop in the tarmac road and head towards Frandy Burn. A suitable crossing point normally exists just before the burn meets the River Devon, but this crossing is subject to suitable water levels, and when the burn is in spate it is advisable to return to the start point by remaining on the road.

Once across the burn a flat section of easy ground contours right the way round the bottom of Berry Hill. Ignoring the option to cross the river, the route runs parallel to the River Devon for 1km, crossing a small burn and meeting a coniferous woodland copse. Pass through this initial woodland, staying next to the river, then entering briefly onto open ground before encountering mixed deciduous woodland. Walk through the woodland by the river for 100m to arrive at the stone bridge and private road 400m from the start of the route.

WALK 16
The Glendevon Reservoirs

Distance	13.4km
Height gain	479m
Time	3hr 30min
Difficulty rating	4
Maps required	OS Landranger 58 (1:50,000)
	OS Explorer 366 (1:25,000)
	Harvey's Map – Ochil Hills (1:25,000)
Start point	turning for Frandy Fishery (GR948053)

The broad moorland hills surrounding the Upper and Lower Glendevon reservoirs offers a sense of isolation and solitude unrivalled in the Ochils. The wide diversity of bird and plant life at the edges of the upper reservoir gives added appeal to this area of the range.

The flat, featureless and often windswept tops, however, can also seem remote and very bleak, and with a lack of any real paths on the first section of this route, navigation is very difficult, requiring skilled micron-avigation in poor weather. Thick tussocks and damp peat sections mean conditions underfoot are also generally challenging until the path is reached at Glen Bee. As such this circular walk is best only undertaken with plenty of time in fine weather.

Take the turning off the A823 for Frandy Fishery and park in the lay-by just after the blue-painted bridge. From the lay-by head westerly up the bank directly opposite, and without any path ascend the slopes of Common Hill.

The slope rises quite gently over short and easy tussocks, reaching a small rib of rock that precedes a small pool and boggy section of ground that is the unas-suming top of Common Hill (412m). From this point on navigation becomes challenging, even in fine weather, and although a general route can be distinguished along the middle of the very broad ridge, it is advisable to aim towards definite features where possible, and estimate location in relation to contour lines.

At the pool on Common Hill aim towards the head of Meadow Burn to reach a distinctive narrow col. From this col head northwards for approximately 300m over increasingly deeper tussocks, with views of the lower reservoir to the southwest and Glen Eagles to the north. Without any landmarks to indicate a change in direction, gradually veer northwesterly, staying in the middle of the hill but still ascending very gradually, reaching an increased gradient near Hawkescraig Burn that leads to the unmarked top of Wether Hill (503m). Despite being the highest point of the walk, views are by no means panoramic, with only distant views of the Strathearn Valley northwards adding to the sense of isolation on these tops.

From the top of Wether Hill head west to cross the drystone dyke and continue towards the finger-like col that is the watershed for Dow Burn. Cross this col at the more shallow northern end, and ascend southwesterly across a small top to another narrow col before moving northwesterly again for approximately 400m to some small rocky outcrops amongst the grass at the top of Craigentaggert Hill (493m).

Descend from the top directly due west to reach either a track or a path that the track merges into. Conditions underfoot improve at this point as the track is followed southeasterly towards the upper reservoir. Cross the burn and the two fences, first at a large wooden ladder and then at a stile. The path continues along the banks of the reservoir, at which point a wide

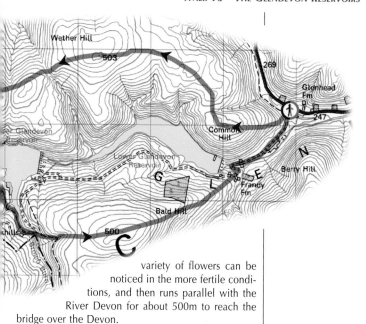

variety of flowers can be noticed in the more fertile conditions, and then runs parallel with the River Devon for about 500m to reach the bridge over the Devon.

Cross the bridge and remain on the path as it doubles back along the river, passing a sign that requests walkers to stay parallel to the reservoir. Although not always distinct, the path skirts around the side of the reservoir, and is certainly the most pleasant section of the walk. ▸

The approach to Backhills can be muddy in parts, in particular when crossing the burns, but the path soon rejoins solid track after passing just below the farm buildings, and then crosses Broich Burn on a wide bridge. After the bridge turn right instead of following the track, and after approximately 50m (well before passing a burn on the left) head east up the bank, gaining height for a distance of approximately 300m before encountering indistinct vehicle tracks, which can be followed upwards for approximately 200m before it is more useful to just head directly towards the top of this unnamed peak (500m).

There is a good opportunity here to spot a variety of birdlife, including waterfowl and raptors such as osprey and hen harriers.

Above Lower Glendevon Reservoir

Vague sheep tracks are discovered and lost, and there is no really useful path to be found until past the top of the hill, where a small but distinct path can be found heading northeasterly off the hill towards Bald Hill, then becoming an obvious track that leads directly to Frandy Farm. On reaching the farm, go through the gates to bypass any sheep pens, and find the tarmac road after passing a small copse of Scots pine and a farmhouse.

Remain on the tarmac road as it loops downhill and then crosses a fine stone bridge at the outlet for the lower reservoir. This road continues for another 1km, leading to the start point of the walk.

WALK 17
Steele's Knowe and Eastbow Hill

Distance	10km
Height gain	240m
Time	2hr 30min
Difficulty rating	2
Maps required	OS Landranger 58 (1:50,000)
	OS Explorer 366 (1:25,000)
	Harvey's Map – Ochil Hills (1:25,000)
Start point	lay-bys at Whitens (GR971053)

Located at the northern reaches of the Ochils, Steele's Knowe and Eastbow Hill are the last points of any real height before the land slips down towards the Strathearn Valley. Although the peaks lack a sense of dramatic height gain and are hardly distinguishable from the surrounding moorland, except for the trig points located on each summit, the landscape here has a very appealing sense of remoteness and isolation.

Despite the generally featureless terrain of this part of the Ochils, navigation is significantly aided by linear features for the first two-thirds of this circular walk. After this careful navigation is required from Eastbow Hill only in the worst of weather.

Parking is available in a couple of large lay-bys just after the Forestry Commission road at Whitens (GR971053) on the A823. From here walk westwards for just under 1km and the route begins properly by solitary Hunthall Cottage.

Go through the gate next to the cottage and cross diagonally through the small meadow to the small copse in the opposite corner by the burn. Cross carefully through the brittle farm gate and ascend, without any defined path, up the bank, through a sprinkling of gorse bushes, onto the obvious spur of Hillkitty. Proceed uphill

on this spur, with the ground peppered with visible patches of rock, through the grass, until a small cairn is reached as the ground levels out after the initial ascent.

From here the route to Steele's Knowe is very simple (even in low visibility), as a drystone dyke that leads practically all the way to Steele's Knowe summit soon comes into view shortly after the cairn. Stay parallel to the dyke, heading in a general northerly direction for roughly 2.5km. Grassy quad tracks run parallel to the dyke, providing easy going underfoot.

Around 0.5km directly south of Steele's Knowe recent construction work has begun on windfarms not yet marked on maps. Access to Steele's Knowe can be made by carefully crossing or by-passing the works' access path (not marked on the map). A lonely trig point marks the summit of Steele's Knowe (485m).

The land slopes away gradually northwards from here, so there is not a great deal of view in the immediate foreground, with the Strathearn Valley not yet completely visible, but there are fine views of the hills directly north.

Leaving the trig point, head directly west for 500m to where a wire fence meets an old drystone dyke and fence. Cross over the new fence and back onto the quad tracks. With the wire fence on the right-hand side, and after initially passing through a gate and past a small communications mast, stay on the quad tracks as they head in a westerly direction, over good, level ground for just over 1km, to reach another fence and gate at Jamie's Grain. This section of the walk is perhaps the most pleasant, as despite being essentially featureless moorland, the complete absence of any visible roads or buildings for miles around contributes to a real sense of wilderness rarely bettered in the Ochils.

Storm clouds over the isolated peak of Steele's Knowe

Once through the gate, the terrain over the next 700m to the summit of Eastbow is more difficult. In amongst some quite well-established heather are several bogs and drainage channels, so the easiest course to follow is to stay as close to the drystone dyke as possible until the terrain becomes more favourable, nearer the summit of Eastbow Hill (476m) marked by a trig point. ◄

Without the aid of a path or linear feature, leave Eastbow Hill initially in a southerly direction to reach the col between Eastbow and East Craigs. The best point to aim for is the western side of the col (600m from Eastbow summit), where the ground slopes away significantly to Corryuby Gully, as even in claggy conditions this change in the inclination of ground should be obvious.

Just after the col, and still heading in a southerly direction, move onto the grassy quad track that soon becomes visible, leading past an initial cairn that marks the slightly higher point on East Craigs (473m), then close by a larger cairn that, perversely, marks a slightly lower spot-height. Stay on the quad track as it follows the line of the broad hill, bending east and then continuing briefly in a southern direction to the Seat, reaching a gate in the fence that leads down to Thatch Burn.

Shortly after passing through the gate the quad track splits on Truffy Knowe. The left track should be followed, becoming faint in parts but essentially descending the tapering spur on its north side with the burn just to the right. At the bottom of Truffy Knowe spur a rough farm track is met that leads all the way out towards Kaimknowe Farm. Once at the farm stay on the track above the farm buildings and descend around and past the farm sheds, passing through a metal gate then turning right to descend onto the A823, after which it is approximately a 1.5km walk back to the parking spot. Despite walking this final section along the road, it is often a surprisingly good place to spot wildlife, as roe deer can often be seen on the hills on the other side of the River Devon, and the river itself attracts a wide variety of birdlife – resident herons as well as numerous oyster-catchers.

Of the two hills, the view from Eastbow is far more impressive, with a wide panorama of the Strathearn Valley and the hills behind; particularly noticeable are Ben Vorlich and Stuc a' Chroin to the west.

WALK 18
Ben Thrush Circuit

Distance	6km
Height gain	264m
Time	1hr 40min
Difficulty rating	2
Maps required	OS Landranger 58 (1:50,000)
	OS Explorer 366 (1:25,000)
	Harvey's Map – Ochil Hills (1:25,000)
Start point	youth hostel (GR989046)

Ideal for a quick, uncomplicated walk that includes some good views, this circular route has easy access from the roadside, which means the summit of Ben Thrush can be easily reached within 20 minutes of leaving the car.

Route finding is relatively simple over generally good terrain, but in bad weather navigation can be slightly tricky after leaving Ben Thrush, and the lack of a defined path from the Long Craig shoulder means an exit needs to be found through the woods at Glendevon Castle.

Park at the lay-by just in front of the youth hostel off the A823 (GR989046). Head through the gate and along the track, passing the youth hostel to the right to reach the buildings at Glenfoot after 300m. From here go through the gate as the path forks, and ascend gradually along a muddy track that soon becomes a firm path, joining the farm track from Borland on the left.

Continue along this farm track until the end of the drystone dyke, turning left off the track and following the line of the dyke as it climbs more steeply uphill until the corner dyke is reached. Head in the same direction, and then past the small but obvious disused quarry to reach the summit of Ben Thrush (456m). ▶

Similar to other hills in the immediate area, Ben Thrush has a pleasant, small and rounded summit with good views across to neighbouring peaks.

A faint path leads in a northerly direction from the summit, eventually running parallel to a fenceline that provides a useful navigational handrail to the mast at GR986069. Recent windfarm construction work in this area has created an access road in the glen between Long Craig and Ben Thrush (not marked on the map). The top section of the access path will need to be carefully crossed or by-passed to reach the point at 474m. Once near the mast, and before the fence is joined by another fence to the right, cross the fence and move northwesterly across more tussocky terrain for just under 500m, before veering almost directly south to move onto the broad ridge of Long Craig. Once on the ridge and heading southwesterly, faint quad tracks should be visible, and provide easier conditions underfoot until the point of descent from Long Craig.

Continuing in the same direction, descend down the middle of the shoulder to the point where the two dykes meet perpendicularly to each other (GR977056). Head left and follow the ramshackle dyke across and downhill, with the easiest exit through the woods at GR978055. As no clear path exists here, a 'route of best fit' needs to be picked through the trees before shortly reaching the Glendevon Castle road just as it bends and descends to the A832.

On reaching the main road turn left and continue on the narrow pathway on the opposite side of the road for 1.5km, passing a fine stone bridge over the River Devon before reaching the start point of the walk.

WALK 19
Glendevon Forest Circuit

Distance	18.3km
Height gain	1188m
Time	5hr 40min
Difficulty rating	4
Maps required	OS Landranger 58 (1:50,000)
	OS Explorer 366 (1:25,000)
	OS Explorer 369 (1:25,000)
	Harvey's Map – Ochil Hills (1:25,000)
Start point	Castlehill Reservoir car park (GR002028)

This long, circular walk over a series of small but defined hills feels more reminiscent of the rolling landscape of the Scottish Borders than the typical steep-sided moorland of the Ochils. Viewpoints abound on this route, with the vast eastern panorama from Mellock Hill spectacular enough to rival views from anywhere else in the range.

Largely untouched by walkers, the majority of these hills do not have paths across them, which means that in brief sections the going underfoot and route finding will be tricky. However, for the most part linear features such as forest boundaries and fences, as well as obvious distinctions in the landscape, mean macronavigation is simple in all but the worst weather, and a sense of solitude is guaranteed.

Start at the Castlehill Reservoir car park just off the A823 (take note at the entrance of the time at which the gates of the car park will be closed).

From the car park, cross the reservoir walkway, with some vertigo-inducing drops down the side of the dam wall on the right, and then ascend on the path that bends round to the left, passing through a wooden boxfence, and after a couple of minutes a metal gate with a gravel track just ahead. As the path reaches the gravel track, pass over the fence and into the field, heading towards the cluster of Scots pines.

Proceed uphill without a path, but over easy ground, crossing another fence and reaching the summit of Easter Downhill (361m), marked by a large cairn which itself is in the middle of the ruins of a hill fort, the foundations of which are still clearly visible, and which

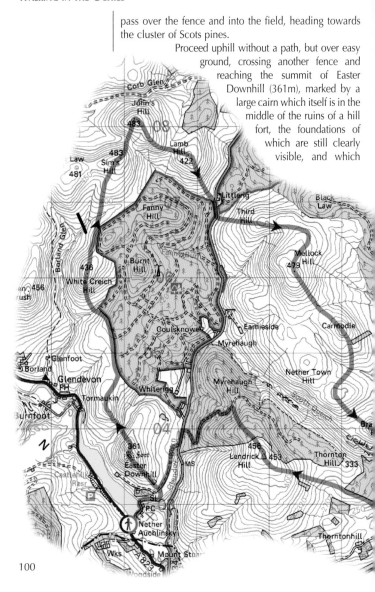

Seamab from Easter Downhill

encompass almost the entirety of the small summit. Excellent views from the summit owe more to the hill's pronounced isolation than its modest height, nevertheless the all-round panorama includes Seamab Hill directly south across the reservoir, Innerdownie to the west, and to the north and east a great view of the route ahead along the tops around and above Glendevon Forest.

Descend Easter Downhill in a northerly direction without the aid of a path, but staying on the obvious spur until a fence is reached after approximately 200m. Turn left and follow the fence steeply downhill to cross a drystone dyke, and ascend northwesterly to the summit of Tormaukin (335m), at which point the defensive advantages of building a fort on top of steep-sided Easter Downhill become clear.

From the unmarked top of Tormaukin move north towards the edge of the Glendevon Forest and continue north, staying next to the forest fenceline for just under 1km before descending to a small burn and a drystone dyke. Cross the burn and the dyke and head directly north, uphill to the small, rounded summit of White Creich Hill (436m), marked up a collection of stones and again providing excellent views.

View of the Innerdownie Ridge

From the top, head north again and back to the edge of the forest on Black Creich Hill, where a faint path can be discerned. Stay on this path next to the forest, and as the fence and forest bend round to the right, maintain the route directly north, descending to cross the burn (this area can be boggy at times) before ascending gradually, still in a northerly direction, to the top of Sim's Hill (483m), where a fence is met. Follow the line of the fence northeasterly, descending quite steeply to an obvious col, and ascend north for a distance of 250m to the relatively large and flat summit of John's Hill (483m).

Descend gradually from John's Hill on a faint path that leads southeasterly, to reach a small col before ascending to Lamb Hill, from which point descend in a continued southeasterly direction to reach the corner of the forest by the B934 road, adjacent to a white house. Pass through the metal gate by the gorse bushes opposite the house and turn right on meeting the road.

Continue south along the road for approximately 200m, and just after the road begins to bend, go through the farm gate on the left-hand side at the start of the field. After crossing the small burn, begin to gradually ascend Third Hill in a easterly direction, after 600m meeting faint vehicle tracks that lead directly to the broad summit. As the ground flattens at the top of Third Hill the route visibly doglegs around off the vehicle track to ascend Mellock Hill without any clear waymarkers, apart from a fence that bisects the ridge and the top of the hill.

Cross over the fence to reach the highest, yet unmarked, point of Mellock Hill (479m), and an immediately impressive panorama presents itself. ▸

On leaving Mellock Hill two ridges fork left and right, with Cloon Burn running in between. Descend towards the most obvious next summit, the small lump that is Carmodle, on the left-hand ridge. Going underfoot becomes quite boggy in this section on wet days, without any alternative route around (crossing over to Nether Town Hill is probably worse).

Once over Carmodle, descend almost directly south, soon walking parallel to a drystone dyke that meets the fence by the Cloon Burn (GR031048). Cross the fence and stay with the dyke for approximately 400m to pass through the gate at the col between Nether Town and Broadhead. Move easily southeasterly over Broadhead and descend with the fenceline to below Braughty Hill, which itself is then quickly ascended and then descended to the gate at GR040036.

On a clear day this is easily one of the finest views in the Ochils, as the Lomond Hills rise dramatically from the flat alluvial plain, looming over the huge expanse of Loch Leven, beyond which can be seen the Firth of Forth, and in the far distance North Berwick Law, the Bass Rock and the North Sea.

The village of Glendevon

From this point route finding becomes difficult until the slopes of Lendrick Hill are reached, with a series of annoying obstacles hampering any easy walking. Pass through the gate and follow the next fence downhill for 100m before crossing through another gate. Follow the treeline at the edge of the field down towards South Quiech Burn, where the best crossing point for the shallow burn is just before the tributary burn at the end of the forest (GR040034).

Climb the bank after the burn and stay parallel with the edge of the forest for just over 1km, over difficult and sometimes frustrating terrain, before reaching easier ground at a farm track at GR036026. Take this track as it moves into the small section of forest and crosses Cross Burn, leaving it in the open ground just as it bends back into the forest.

From here continue uphill in a northwesterly direction with the forest on the right, soon reaching a fence from where a continuation in the same direction for another 1km leads to the top of Lendrick Hill, marked first with a trig point (453m) and then with a smaller cairn slightly higher up (456m). ◄

Fine views are again afforded from the summit, which is the most popular peak in this area of the Ochils.

To descend from the top, follow a faint grassy path from the cairn in a vague northerly direction to cross a fence into the forestry section, from where a waymarking post can be seen in the firebreak immediately ahead. Descend steeply from the post straight down the firebreak, turning left on the forestry track to arrive at a car park on the B934 after about 10 minutes.

Turning left from the car park, continue along the road for approximately 200m, and just before the road bends and dips, cross at the bridge on the right to move onto a rough track which circles around the bottom of Easter Downhill. With the cluster of Scots pines on the side of the hill as a landmark, walk around the hill until a grassy track forks to the left (in line with a fence that runs to the Scots pines), which is the original route on to Easter Downhill. Descend this track back to the reservoir car park.

WALK 20
The Round of Nine

Distance	25.5km
Height gain	1120m
Time	7hr
Difficulty rating	4
Maps required	OS Landranger 57 (1:50,000)
	OS Landranger 58 (1:50,000)
	OS Explorer 366 (1:25,000)
	Harvey's Map – Ochil Hills (1:25,000)
Start point	Menstrie (GR851971)

The locally known 'Round of Nine' is the classic lateral Ochil traverse, covering all the 'Donald' peaks in the range. (The inclusion of the Law in the Round of Nine is a cause of much debate, as it is considered by many not to achieve Donald status, although it is a fine hill in its own right.)

This long, and at times challenging, point-to-point walk is the ideal way to enjoy a high-level exploration of the differing characteristics of the Ochils' largest peaks. Covering a distance of over 25km, the route encounters demanding terrain as well as sections where accurate navigation skills will be necessary, and as such is suitable only for those confident in their hillcraft and fitness.

The route can be made in either direction, but the one described here is west to east, so as to deal with the most difficult terrain and tricky navigational sections early on, and also to finish the walk at the Tormaukin Inn at Glendevon. Two cars will be needed, as public transport back from Glendevon is infrequent.

The walk starts from the west end of Menstrie. Take Park Road off the A91 at the Holly Tree pub and park at the row of cottages just after the road bends round. At the end of the cottages a footpath sign on a telephone pole marks a vehicle track that starts after the wooden stile.

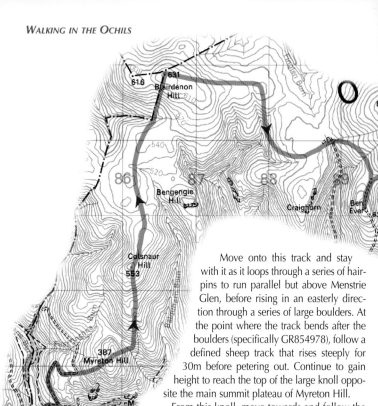

Move onto this track and stay with it as it loops through a series of hairpins to run parallel but above Menstrie Glen, before rising in an easterly direction through a series of large boulders. At the point where the track bends after the boulders (specifically GR854978), follow a defined sheep track that rises steeply for 30m before petering out. Continue to gain height to reach the top of the large knoll opposite the main summit plateau of Myreton Hill.

From this knoll, move towards and follow the drystone dyke that ascends towards Myreton's top. On reaching the flatter ground of Myreton's summit, cross over the dyke to the cairn for good views south. To proceed with the route, cross back over and follow the dyke for just over 200m, then cross back over again before it bends sharply to descend to Lethen Burn. With the dyke now on the left-hand side, cross Lethen Burn and ascend right on a thin but visible path for a distance of approximately 130m to arrive on a narrow spur that leads from the Colsnaur ridge.

Proceed up this spur, shortly crossing a wire fence and drystone dyke at GR862984. A vague path continues along this spur and is soon joined by another fence to the right, which draws closer to the path on the approach to the distinctive summit of Colsnaur Hill (553m), marked by a large

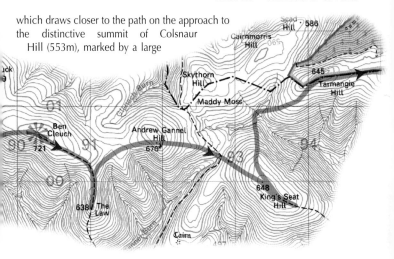

Map continues p.108

cairn and wooden post. A wide trench next to the summit cairn provides excellent shelter from westerly winds.

The route from Colsnaur now continues directly to the most westerly Donald in the Ochils and the first Donald of the walk, Blairdenon. While navigation is simple for this section, as the route simply follows the fenceline all the way to Blairdenon summit, the terrain starts to become more difficult as the obvious quad tracks that initially lead away from Colsnaur disappear in the boggy ground of Menstrie Moss. Going underfoot improves somewhat after the short ascent to the flat and unremarkable summit of Blairdenon (631m), where the only real views are north, with a particularly good profile of Ben Vorlich and Stuc a' Chroin.

Moving on from Blairdenon, cross the fence that has just been followed at its intersection with another fence on the summit point of the hill, and gently descend due east over good ground to the gate in the fenceline at GR879016. A bearing will definitely need to be taken in poor weather, as this section of the walk enters a featureless and navigationally difficult area of the Ochils.

Once at the gate the next navigational attack point is the top of the vehicle track as it crosses Benbuck Burn at GR889009, but the direct route from the gate crosses a large area of bogs and sodden peat hags, which is particularly hazardous after prolonged wet conditions. Unfortunately, a route to Ben Ever completely avoiding this terrain is practically impossible without first descending steep slopes into Birken Glen and clambering back up via the Craighorn ridge.

It is best to go round the edge of this boggy area by heading in a southerly direction from the gate, and following the direction of the East Cameron Burn by staying roughly 40m higher than and parallel to it, until its intersection with the other burn (with no name) from the south. Follow the course of the burn with no name uphill as it leads up to its watershed on the flat area 400m north of Craighorn summit. The large mass of Ben Cleuch should now be clearly visible, as well as adjoining Ben Buck and Ben Ever, and a course is now easily taken over improving ground to the top of the vehicle track at GR889009. ◄

To reach Ben Ever from the track, start to ascend the grassy slope just after the Benbuck

With the most demanding terrain and navigation completed, the rest of the route becomes comparatively simple and enjoyable.

Burn, and continue in a southeasterly direction for just under 700m to arrive at the intersection of three fences on the distinct col. Cross the fence at the stile and follow the obvious path as it ascends gradually in a southerly direction for just over 300m to reach the unassuming summit of Ben Ever (622m), where the actual top is slightly higher than both of the small collections of stones.

Double back to the col and cross the stile onto the obvious path that ascends quite steeply and parallel to the fence for 500m, before bending round to gently approach the highest point in the Ochils, Ben Cleuch (721m). The flat but bouldery summit provides excellent all-round views, although it can also be very cold in windy weather, which has prompted the construction of a large, ramshackle shelter cairn. Leave Ben Cleuch on the defined path as it descends gradually in a southeasterly direction, and stay on the path as it bends round to run parallel to the new fence heading due south to the Law (638m). ▶

From the small cairn on the Law go back in the same direction to where the path bent round and cross the stile at the intersection of the fences at GR910003. Again, an obvious path dips and then rises over a distance of just under 1km to reach the summit of Andrew Gannel Hill (670m). The actual top is located next to the fence, but the best views down towards the Gannel Burn are from the small crag at the front of the peak, where the path actually leads towards.

Continuing from Andrew Gannel Hill on the still visible path, the steady descent leads to the watershed at the top of the Gannel Burn after just under 1km. Cross the small burn and then the fence and ascend, without a path, the initially steep and tussocky northwest flank of King's Seat Hill, passing a small scree patch to then come up and onto the tabletop summit of the hill. A path is once again visible from the western end of the plateau,

The Law is the only peak over 600m on this walk not listed as a Donald, a point of much debate, but it is still worthy of inclusion on this walk.

*King's Seat from
Whitewisp Hill*

and may be taken to the shelter cairn at the eastern end for the best views from this peak. However, the actual summit point (648m) is a modest pile of stones at this near end.

As the path forks at the western end of the hill, just by the small summit marker, take the most northerly fork to descend steeply but manageably on the hill's northern spur directly to the junction of two burns at the head of the Glen of Sorrow. Cross the first burn above the rock-pool where the two burns meet and head upstream for 10–15m for the best place to cross the second burn.

From this point, without a path but on fairly good ground, ascend the southwestern shoulder of Tarmangie Hill, until the corner of the boundary fence and drystone dyke come into view. By heading towards the boundary fence a path soon becomes evident, and should be taken as it runs parallel to the dyke along the defined ridge to Tarmangie Hill summit (645m).

Cross the fence to get to the cairn at the summit of the hill, and now the sixth Donald of the walk. As the opposite King's Seat enjoyed the best views south on the route, by contrast this hill provides some of the best views north, to a jagged outline of Highland mountains after the Strathearn Valley.

Leave the cairn at Tarmangie, following a faint path over continuing good ground, that first crosses back over the boundary fence before crossing another fence to enter onto the broad, flat summit of Whitewisp Hill (643m), marked by a large central cairn at the intersection of several faint paths. From the choices of path available at the cairn, take the thin path that heads in a roughly northeasterly direction (a bearing maybe required in poor weather), to arrive at the ladder in the deer-fence next to the intersection of three fences at GR955016. Cross over the ladder and continue along the defined grassy track, keeping the fence on the left.

Attention is required 150–200m after crossing the ladder, as at least two large bogs half covered in vegetation lie across the route of the path. With the path and fence cutting the middle of the ridge all the way to the summit of Innerdownie, and with solid, even ground underfoot, this is a pleasant stroll to the final Donald of the route.

The view north from Whitewisp Hill

The summit of Innerdownie (610m) is marked by a cairn, and 15m before the cairn a pleasant place to stop is the excellent, weather-protected shelter built next to a rock slab.

> With all the peaks completed, the finish point for this walk is the Tormaukin Inn in Glendevon, although an alternative route from this point back to Dollar is also possible. It involves retracing the route back to Whitewisp summit cairn and descending southeasterly along the broad eastern flank to reach the vehicle track at at the edge of Hillfoot Hill forest, which then descends gradually for just over 1km to arrive at the car park for Castle Campbell. From here the road leads back into Dollar. Frequent public transport from the main road through Dollar provides a return to the start point in Menstrie.

Continuing on to Glendevon, leave the summit of Innerdownie in a northeasterly direction, keeping to the obvious path as it initially gradually descends along the ridge to reach Glenquey Hill, where a further steeper but shorter descent reaches a grassy vehicle track as it contours the base of the hill.

Cross the farm track and pass through a large gate in the deer-fence, meeting a tarmac road at Burnfoot. Cross the pretty stone bridge and immediately turn left through the wooden gate, crossing a field to arrive at the metal bridge that crosses the River Devon. After the bridge climb the few steps to the main road through Glendevon, and continue right for 100m to see the welcome sight of the Tormaukin Inn marking the end of the walk.

CAMPSIE FELLS

Few other places in the country can rival the contrast, felt in the Campsie Fells, between being somewhere wild and remote, and yet so close to such a large urban area. Situated just north of Glasgow, the Campsie Fells are an extensive plateau of high ground, bounded by a steep southern escarpment, dramatic crags in the north and the large Carron Valley Reservoir in the east.

The Campsie Fells are the largest range in a cluster of geologically linked hills that includes the Kilpatrick Hills to the southwest and the Fintry and Gargunnock Hills in the northeast, separated from the fells by Blane Water and Endrick Water respectively.

While seven of the nine routes in this section lie within the strict definitions of the Campsie Fells, the walk to Stronend (**Walk 28**) and the North Third Reservoir route (**Walk 29**) are also considered worthy inclusions. Despite lacking the number of established routes of the Ochils, and having only a few defined peaks, the shapely hills of Meikle Bin (**Walk 25**), Dungoil (**Walk 24**), and most notably Dumgoyne (**Walk 21**), combine with spectacular walks around the corries of the northern escarpment to provide the walker with a more than satisfying variety of landscape to explore. Even popular moorland hills such as Cort-Ma Law and Lecket Hill (**Walk 23**) provide a wonderful sense of isolation with some superb views.

The southern boundary of the Campsie Fells is clearly defined by the A891, which links the easily accessible towns of Strathblane, Lennoxtown, Milton of Campsie and Kilsyth, all of which are ideal points from which to begin walks. To the north the pretty town of Fintry is a great base to explore the truly impressive Corrie of Balglass (**Walk 26**) and Little Corrie (**Walk 27**), and is easily reached by an enjoyable drive across the fells on the B822.

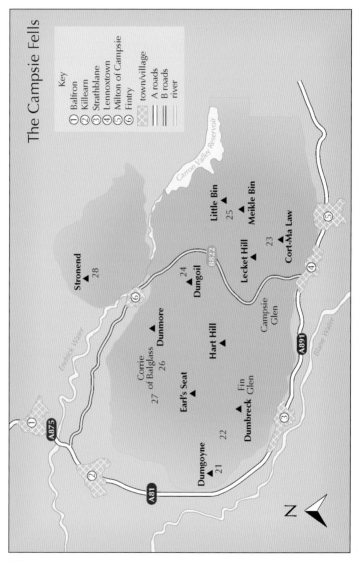

The Campsie Fells

Key

① Balfron
② Killearn
③ Strathblane
④ Lennoxtown
⑤ Milton of Campsie
⑥ Fintry

⬡ town/village
══ A roads
═══ B roads
∿ river

Carron Valley Reservoir

Little Bin
25 ▲
Meikle Bin

Lecket Hill
23 ▲
Cort-Ma Law

Stronend
28 ▲

B822

Dungoil
24 ▲

Campsie Glen

A891

Dunmore
26 ▲

Hart Hill
▲

Corrie
27 of Balglass

Earl's Seat
▲

Fin
Glen

22
Dumbreck
Glen ▲

Dumgoyne
21 ▲

A81

A875

Endrick Water

Blane Water

N

WALK 21
Dumgoyne

Distance	9km
Height gain	387m
Time	2hr 25min
Difficulty rating	2
Maps required	OS Landranger 64 (1:50,000)
	OS Explorer 348 (1:25,000)
	Harvey's Map – Glasgow Popular Hills (1:25,000)
Start point	war memorial, Blanefield (GR556796)

At the southwestern edge of the Campsie Fells the unique, conical-shaped Dumgoyne and the smaller surrounding hills are clear evidence of the volcanic formation of this range. Dumgoyne, itself a volcanic plug, is understandably the most popular hill in the Campsies, due to its easy access from the roadside and its fine, dramatic profile.

After an initial walk-in, the route becomes a circular loop that first includes the opposite and less visited peak of Dumfoyn, from where the best view of the sheer aspect of Dumgoyne's eastern face is seen. The route then ascends Dumgoyne via the steep but manageable northeast face, and descends past Blairgar Wood to reach a farm track that rejoins the original walk-in route. Apart from the section on Dumfoyn, paths exist for all of the route, making navigation easy and going underfoot generally good. Some steep but manageable slopes may prove unsettling for some.

The walk begins from Blanefield. Park off the main road (A81) by the war memorial (GR556796) (parking can be limited here at times).

Walk ahead in a northwesterly direction along the hedged, tarmac road for approximately 300m, before the road becomes a track that reaches a large, black, metal gate leading into open ground. There are good views ahead of the two peaks of Dumgoyne and Dumfoyn, fine views also to the left, including the entirely wooded, domed hill of Dumgoyach, and to the right, the steep escarpment of the Strathblane Hills.

Continue along this straight and solid track for approximately 1.25km, passing a series of small burns and crossing through three more gates before reaching a very broad, stone bridge then a smaller metal-fenced bridge within some trees. Cross over the bridge, and just before reaching the second, larger metal-fenced bridge (next to the farm gate), as the track begins to bend, head through the swing gate and start to ascend on an initially grassy, broad path running parallel to the coniferous plantation of Craigbrock Wood on the left. As the path forks opposite the top of the Craigbrock Wood, take the left-hand path that becomes narrower and more muddy in parts, eventually crossing the burn at Cauldhame Glen.

Immediately after the burn, cross the stile and continue along the obvious path, with Dumfoyn rising directly into view on the right. Just as Dumgoyne comes into view leave the path, turning right onto the steep grassy slopes (GR545824).

The walk into Dumgoyne and Dumfoyne

Ascending quite steeply, but only for a height of approximately 50m, the ground becomes quite rocky, with some small crags that can easily be manoeuvred past, to arrive at more level ground on the short ridge that leads directly to the unmarked and flat summit of Dumfoyn (426m). From the small tabletop summit the best view of the Dumgoyne's dramatic east face is seen.

From Dumfoyn continue directly north, still without any clear path but over easy ground, to reach Drumiekill Knowes after 300m, then descend due east over some craggy then damp ground for 400m to reach the narrow but obvious path that picks its way steeply but safely up the northeast face of Dumgoyne. ▶

To leave Dumgoyne, follow the path southwesterly as it descends along the centre of the ridge then curves to avoid some craggy drops. Descend to the point where a long patch of scree is obvious, and continue downhill more steeply alongside this scree on an obvious path to eventually flatter (and boggier) ground facing two stiles. Once over both stiles, continue along the path across the open field for 300m to reach the farm track and a large black gate. Pass through the gate and follow the track as it initially heads in a southerly direction through mixed woodland.

The summit of Dumgoyne (427m) is a modest, flat area marked by a large stone that was recently helicoptered into position by the Strathendrick Rotarians. The excellent views to island-studded Loch Lomond, the Arrocher Alps and Ben Lomond attract numerous visitors on clear days.

The defined and craggy shape of Dumgoyne

Remain on this track for the next 2km and take the left-hand route when the track forks at the end of Parkhill Wood, passing a small white cottage before returning to the two bridges from where the initial entrance to the hills was made, thus completing the loop. Head back to Blanefield by returning the 2km along the track that was used to walk in.

WALK 22
Ballagan Burn Circuit

Distance	11km
Height gain	500m
Time	3hr
Difficulty rating	3
Maps required	OS Landranger 64 (1:50,000)
	OS Landranger 57 (1:50,000)
	OS Explorer 348 (1:25,000)
	Harvey's Map – Glasgow Popular Hills (1:25,000)
Start point	track to Leddriegreen House (GR565798)

This relatively long walk starts at the southern edge of the Campsie Fells, but crosses the western edge of the range to include the spectacular panorama at its northern escarpment. The walk loops around the long slice of the Ballagan Burn Glen on two broad, parallel ridges, reaching the highest point in the Campsie Fells, Earl's Seat (578m), at the halfway point.

Despite there being no established paths on this route, the going underfoot, although at times awkward, is for the most part unchallenging. The lack of major navigational features on the first half of the walk, however, does mean route finding can be difficult in poor visibility.

The walk starts from the track leading to Leddriegreen House (GR565798), but as this is a private road it is best to park in the nearby cul-de-sac, Dunglass View, which is the next turning west off the A891.

From the cul-de-sac, cross the fence to reach the private road to Leddriegreen House, and immediately cross another fence (unfortunately there are no gates or stiles here) and enter into the field above Broadgate. Cross the field in a northeasterly direction, aiming to reach the fence by the corner of the small Leddriegreen plantation after approximately 200m. Cross the fence by the plantation and begin to head steadily uphill, without any visible path, towards the obvious rocky outcrop marked as Wangie on the map (Explorer). Although the ground is soggy in parts and steepens towards the outcrop, it is easily manageable.

The Wangie, meaning a cut or slice, is a smaller version of the Whangie in the neighbouring Kilpatrick Hills. It is a prominent feature on this side of the hill, with several large rocky clefts to the left-hand side and good views across to the volcanic plug, Dunglass. The adventurous walker can also pick out a good scrambling route on less exposed areas of the rock. Only experienced scramblers should attempt climbs here as the drops from the face are large.

The most interesting way around the Wangie is to proceed upwards on the left-hand side, following some visible sheep tracks through the rocky clefts, soon arriving above the outcrop. Continue quite steeply upwards, still without a path but over easy terrain, in a vaguely northeasterly direction until the ground levels out after approximately 200m. Navigation from here on is difficult in low visibility, but aim to reach the small pool, marked as Pool Island on the map (Explorer), and continue along the ridge in a northwesterly direction, keeping more to the right-hand side of the broad ridge and using the slopes down to Ballagan Burn as a rough navigational aid.

After walking 1km from the pool the ground becomes increasingly soft near the watershed for Silver Burn, and with large boggy areas and peat hags to negotiate, conditions underfoot remain tricky for about 1km until Graham's Cairn is reached. From the small circular cairn descend to the col and cross the fence and small burn, looking left for good views down to the volcanic summits of Dumgoyne and Dumfoyne, before rising once more onto the improved ground of the small ridge of Clachertyfarlie Knowes. ▶

Descending northwards off the top spur of Clachertyfarlie Knowes, head towards the obvious rise of Bell Craig, and contour around the east side of this large knoll to reach the metal gate in the fence just before the burn. Cross the minor burn that falls off the northern escarpment of the fells at GR558859 and proceed along the vague grassy quad tracks that head alongside the escarpment, providing some spectacular views. The quad tracks soon pass a large cairn and continue along the Ballagan Tops, with partial views of the Corrie of Balglass and Little Corrie coming into sight.

The strange shape of Dunglass as seen on the start of the Ballagan Burn Loop

At this stage views north really open up, with the hills of the Arrochar Alps and Ben Lomond most prominent.

The unimpeded panorama from Earl's Seat, the highest point in the range, is vast and undoubtedly impressive, with the view north probably one of the best in Central Scotland.

Approximately 400m after passing the cairn, and after skirting some peat hags on the right, a faint track breaks off to the right from the quad tracks and heads southeasterly, soon gently ascending the short distance to the top of Earl's Seat (578m), marked with a cairn and a trig point. ◄

From the summit of Earl's Seat descend in a south-westerly direction, staying next to the fence for approximately 300m until another fence joins on the right. Cross over the summit fence and follow this new fence – on slightly more difficult ground as grass gives way to heather and peat bogs for a short period. Stay near the fence, heading initially to Little Earl, and this will provide the navigational handrail to proceed along the ridge.

The section from Little Earl to Owsen Hill has some of the most difficult terrain on the walk, as boggy peat hags require negotiation for roughly 200m. A large quantity of old, discarded fencing wire is also a hard-to-spot hazard underfoot at this point. From Owsen Hill onwards the going underfoot improves dramatically, reverting back to short grassy tussocks on relatively flat ground and distinct quad tracks. Views of Glasgow soon come back into view, as does the parallel ridge used on the walk-in. Staying on the quad tracks the trig point on Drumbreck (508m) is reached.

After walking 700m from Drumbreck, still using the quad tracks that parallel the fence, a metal gate is reached in an adjoining fence. Instead of going through the gate, turn right and head down the hill, now without a path, following the new fence. The descent becomes quite steep in parts but is manageable, and Ballagan Burn is soon reached, with good views up the glen showing the twisting course of the water.

Cross the burn here at a suitable point. (When the burn is in spate, do not attempt to cross it; instead, cross over the fence and follow the course of the upwards side of the fence that encloses the glen at the Spout of Ballagan to reach Ballagan House and the A891.) Once over, stay on the upward side of the fence that encircles the lower glen, and descend with the fence as it boxes around large drops to reach an old drystone dyke.

Turn right at the dyke and follow it to its corner, continuing down to the nearby gate. From the gate go diagonally across the field to the corner of the forestry at Leddriegreen House, where the initial ascent began. Cross the next field to return to the start of the walk.

The view across to Loch Lomond from the Ballagan Burn route

WALK 23
Cort-Ma Law and Lecket Hill Circuit

Distance	9.8km
Height gain	462m
Time	2hr 45min
Difficulty rating	2
Maps required	OS Landranger 64 (1:50,000)
	OS Explorer 348 (1:25,000)
	Harvey's Map – Glasgow Popular Hills (1:25,000)
Start point	car park at the Clachan of Campsie (GR612795) or off the Crow Road (GR613802)

Starting at picturesque Campsie Glen, the route rises gradually onto a plateaued horseshoe ridge that initially provides excellent views south to Glasgow and beyond. Heading in an anticlockwise direction, the route continues to the peaks of Cort-Ma Law and Lecket Hill before descending back towards the glen. The route is also equally enjoyable walked in the opposite direction.

Despite the featureless character of the moorland landscape, paths are generally obvious on this well-used route, and navigation is therefore relatively simple. Conditions underfoot, however, can be particularly boggy in certain sections, with care required especially between the two peaks. Walking poles are therefore particularly recommended for this route.

Two car parks are available for this route. The lower and smaller car park at the Clachan of Campsie is situated at the bottom of Campsie Glen, and thus allows a very worthwhile exploration of the glen en route to the peaks. The higher and larger car park is off the Crow Road and just above the glen.

From the lower car park, signs indicate the start of Campsie Glen, and after a short walk from the car park on a gravel track a small information point is reached where the path forks. Take the right-hand fork and ascend above the glen, reaching the larger car park and viewpoint after less than 10 minutes. ▸

Crossing over the car park and Crow Road, a visible path leads up the grassy ridge past a concrete bunker and ascends on initially solid grassy terrain mixed with a sprinkling of rock patches. As height and views are gained, the going underfoot becomes soft and boggy in parts (an indication of what lies ahead), but the path is well trodden and visible all the way to Crichton's Cairn, which is reached after just over 1km from the upper car park and marks the end of any further significant ascent. Impressive views south to Glasgow and beyond justify the popularity of this well-visited cairn.

Continuing east from the cairn on the undulating path that now rides along the plateaued ridge, a second cairn is passed which is almost a carbon copy of the first, and by the time a third, smaller cairn is reached the views south are almost lost.

Just before the car park a quick detour left and through the swing gate down to Kirk Burn is recommended, to view the pretty waterfalls at James's Linn.

Before the path bends around northeasterly to Cort-Ma Law there is the option to turn off right (GR648796) on a short path to reach another significant cairn where there are the best views south on this route. From this cairn a path leads south through the crags at Knockybuckle to provide an interesting route to Lennoxtown.

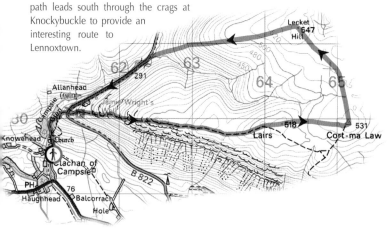

The going underfoot becomes increasingly boggy all the way to the summit point of Cort-Ma Law (531m), marked with a triangulation point. Views from the summit include prominent Meikle Bin and a cairn, just about identifiable, on Lecket Hill.

Leaving Cort-Ma Law, the path forks in two, with the right fork heading in the direction of Meikle Bin; the left fork needs to be taken. While initially obvious, the path soon becomes vague, and in parts particularly boggy. This 1.5km section between the two peaks is the most difficult of the route, and concentration is required to assess the most suitable way through the boggy ground, bearing in mind that the line of the path does not always provide the most solid ground underfoot. Walking poles to test for soft ground ahead are particularly recommended here, but once on the slight incline to Lecket Hill terrain improves significantly. From the cairn at Lecket Hill (547m) there are the best views north on the route, with an impressive collection of peaks framed in the distance between Campsie Muir and Meikle Bin.

Head almost directly due west from Lecket Hill on the obvious path to reach the intersection of three fences. Cross the stile and continue on the path westwardly, along the centre of the flat and occasionally boggy ridge, before descending more steeply to the Crow Road that now comes into view. Cross a small burn and continue down-hill and southwesterly on the road, passing after approximately 1km what at first glance appears to be a small shrine tucked into the right-hand side of the road. ▸

Continue along the road for another 500m to return to the top car park, where a descent back along the initial climb up the glen returns to the lower car park at the Clachan of Campsie, where refreshments are available.

The small structure with an inscribed poem is known as Jamie Wright's Well, and was apparently built by a local angler as a source of refreshment.

Jamie Wright's Well on the Cort-Ma Law circuit

WALK 24
Dungoil

Distance	7.4km
Height gain	229m
Time	1hr 50min
Difficulty rating	1
Maps required	OS Landranger 57 (1:50,000)
	OS Explorer 348 (1:25,000)
	Harvey's Map – Glasgow Popular Hills (1:25,000)
Start point	Crow Road (GR641851)

The steep north face of Dungoil gives this small, isolated peak a sense of presence beyond its actual height. A lack of easy direct access to the summit also adds to the challenge and satisfaction of reaching the airy top.

Entirely encircled by thick and almost impenetrable forestry, there is only one feasible access point through the trees, so this short route is 'there and back' rather than circular, despite the fact that the summit is a return distance of less than 1km to the start point. The quickest method recommended for reaching the summit, therefore, is using a mountain bike to cover the long looping forest track to reach the entry point of the ridge at the back of the hill. Navigation is simple as long as attention is paid to finding the entry point to the ridge.

The route starts where a farm track joins the Crow Road at GR641851. Parking for no more than two cars is available off the road here (account for large farm vehicles being able to access the track).

Cross over the metal gate onto the track and continue gradually uphill, entering the forestry by crossing over another gate. Proceed along the track, heading westwards for 1.5km through dense forestry, with only the occasional glimpse of views northwards, and eventually the track loops back in the opposite direction and soon after arrives at a fork where the left-hand track should be taken.

After 250m another fork in the track appears, and again the left-hand (lower) track should be taken, after which a marshy patch of cleared forestry is seen to the right, marked on the map (Explorer) as a small pond with an island.

Just after this marshy area the track begins to bend slightly, and a small stagnant pond is passed on the left, which is then almost immediately followed by another small patch of cleared forestry, also on the left-hand side, with a sign warning against starting fires. It is at this point that the forestry is at its thinnest, and access to the ridge may be gained through the seemingly impenetrable trees.

Leaving the track, head to the top left corner of the cleared area and a short, narrow route through the trees

Dungoil seen from across the Endrick Water

View to Stronend from the steep slopes of Dungoil

should be visible. Once through the trees and into open ground on the other side there are some small waymarking stones piled on a boulder, and a short and easy scramble is required to reach the grassy path now on the summit ridge of Dungoil. ◄

Breaking onto the open ground of the ridge, after the forest walk, provides instantly satisfying views north to the Fintry Hills, west to Dunmore and east to the crags of Dunbrach.

The faint path initially ascends to reach a small knoll before heading northeast to reach the summit of Dungoil (424m). The north face of the hill has an impressively steep and craggy incline that creates airy views to the forest and the start of the walk below. Due to the lack of firebreaks in the forestry there is no easy exit from the north side of the hill to make the route circular, so the inward route must be followed back to the starting point.

WALK 25
Meikle Bin

Distance	12.6km
Height gain	360m
Time	3hr
Difficulty rating	2
Maps required	OS Landranger 64 (1:50,000)
	OS Landranger 57 (1:50,000)
	OS Explorer 348 (1:25,000)
	Harvey's Map – Glasgow Popular Hills (1:25,000)
Start point	lay-by near north reservoir wall (GR673859)

The name Meikle Bin simply means 'Big Hill', and is vividly descriptive of the most pronounced hill in the Campsie Fells. Visible from almost everywhere in the range, the hill is rendered more distinctive by the smaller adjoining summit of 'Little Bin'.

Situated above the Carron Valley Reservoir and entirely within Forestry Commission land, an initial glance at the OS map for the area would suggest that any route to the summit would entail long, viewless walks through dense woodland. This looping walk, however, is on surprisingly open ground with unimpeded views on almost all of the ascent to the summit, and while the return section does pass through some forestry, the majority runs alongside the picturesque reservoir. The route is predominantly over forestry tracks, so navigation and going underfoot are not difficult.

The walk starts at the large lay-by (limited car parking available) near the north reservoir wall at the entrance to the Forestry Commission track (GR673859) (opposite the entrance to Todholes).

Head past the green barrier and onto the broad track – immediately amongst mixed woodland, the reservoir soon comes into view. Continue along the track as it

Here are fine open views out to the right across to Dungoil, Dunmore and Dunbrach, and ahead the attractive slanting ridge of Meikle Bin with Little Bin in the foreground.

winds and bends for approximately 1.5km until a bridge across the River Carron is reached. Cross the bridge and continue on the track as it soon bends round, ignoring any option to turn left. The track begins on a gradual incline, reaching a fork junction after 700m where the right-hand track is taken on a fairly straight section that gains height gradually. ◀

Stay on this track as it passes Little Bin. (The option to go to the summit of Little Bin is best taken just before crossing the head of Bin Burn at GR666828. The going underfoot is initially rough, but becomes easier after 100m.) The track continues uphill, bending one way and then the other until the flanks of Lecket Hill come into view at GR663828. At this point a noticeable grassy path leads off to the left up into a firebreak in the trees, which after 20m enters back into open ground at the base of the ridge. Stay on the grassy path as it ascends at a steeper but manageable gradient over good terrain for a distance of 700m to reach the summit of Meikle Bin (570m).

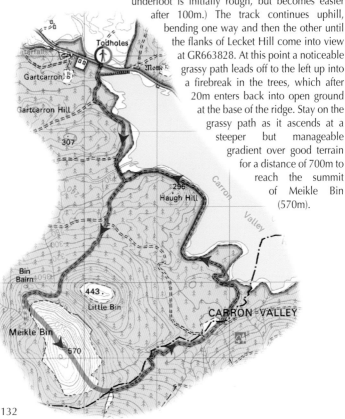

Being the largest hill in the Campsie Fells, and situated in the middle of the range, views are grand and unobstructed. In the immediate foreground to the southwest are the flat moorland and indistinct peaks of Lecket Hill and Cort-Ma Law, with the low ridge line of the Kilsyth Hills (Garrel Hill, Hunt Hill and Tomtain) visible to the southeast. Just below, to the north and east, is the large expanse of the Carron Valley Reservoir, nestled in the broad sweep of forestry, and further north and west are the rugged crags of the Fintry Hills. On clear days from the summit there are fine views stretching out towards the Clyde estuary, with the islands of Arran and Ailsa Craig clearly seen.

Leave the summit following the path in a vague southeasterly direction, quickly reaching a small pool where the path forks. Take the left-hand path and descend over easy ground for 700m to reach a large firebreak at the edge of the forestry. As the path continues into the firebreak, crossing two drainage ditches by means of some slippery railway sleepers, it turns indistinctly left into another firebreak after the second set of sleepers.

Stay on the somewhat vague and muddy path through the firebreak for 400m, before leaving the forestry and crossing a small burn to arrive at the start of a track (GR674816) once more into open ground. Remain on this track as it runs parallel to the burn past Peggie's Spout Waterfall and eventually reaches a junction at GR687823. At this point turning left will create a shorter, though less interesting, loop back to the initial walk-in track.

Continue ahead in the direction of the reservoir, reaching a fork in the track 300m after the junction. Here the less-defined left-hand track that crosses the burn should be taken. This track now loops and turns through dense forestry for approximately 1km before reaching the edge of the reservoir, after which it runs alongside the water before completing the loop as it returns to the original track just up from the bridge over the River Carron. ▸ From the bridge follow the original track back to the car park.

This section near the water's edge is the best part of the walk to observe wildlife. In summer ospreys can occasionally be seen.

WALK 26
The Corrie of Balglass and Earl's Seat

Distance	13.7km
Height gain	483m
Time	3hr 30min
Difficulty rating	4
Maps required	OS Landranger 57 (1:50,000)
	OS Explorer 348 (1:25,000)
	Harvey's Map – Glasgow Popular Hills (1:25,000)
Start point	Fintry (GR616867)

This long, circular route reaches the highest point in the Campsie Fells, Earl's Seat (578m), via one of the most spectacular natural features south of the Highland Fault line – the Corrie of Balglass. The route leaves from the pretty village of Fintry, rising to include the rocky vantage point of Dunmore, before becoming a dramatic cliff-top walk around sheer corrie walls to arrive at Earl's Seat.

While in fine weather the walking on this route is spectacular without being intimidating, large drops at certain points present a real danger on misty or windy days, which is when this walk should be avoided. This walk is not suitable for small children or dogs.

Paths are intermittent, but linear features are used to provide useful navigation, and while the route described is circular, the lack of any real paths leading back from Earl's Seat means that the going underfoot can be heather-strewn, boggy and difficult, in which case returning in the same direction will be the easier option.

The walk starts from the main forked junction in the middle of the pretty village of Fintry, where parking is available on the main road. From the main road, turn into the side road called Dunmore Gardens, and after less than 100m, as the road bends round into the close, continue uphill on what initially appears to be a private road, but is the old access road for the quarry.

Pass by a white house, and the road becomes a track as it enters Fintry Wood with the quarry on the left. Immediately cross the wide but shallow burn and take the left-hand path that briefly runs parallel to the burn until it exits the wood into open ground. Stay on the path as it runs alongside the top of Fintry Wood, before climbing quite steeply for a distance of approximately 300m amongst increasingly bouldery terrain to reach the minor crags below the excellent vantage point of Dunmore. From the cairn at Dunmore the initial view east looks back upon Fintry and Endrick Water, nestled in the narrow valley beneath the wooded and craggy slopes of the Fintry Hills. Further west and north the huge Highland panorama begins to unfold, but is more fully appreciated as the walk continues west from Dunmore.

Fintry
P
PH
Dunmore
Fort
Motte
343
Kilewnan Burn
86
Corrie of Balglass
420
478
488
Allanrowie
's Seat
78

Now without a clear path, continue from Dunmore to cross Kilewnan Burn, opposite an obvious gap in the electrified fence on the other side of the burn. Proceed easily, but with caution, through the gap in the fence, and head south next to the fence for the next 200m to reach a drystone dyke which is then followed for 900m in a westerly direction, passing an obvious knoll at GR601862 to arrive at the edge of the Corrie of Balglass as the dyke ends.

In full view now is the huge 'punchbowl' corrie, a perfectly shaped and deep horseshoe formation with the main burn cutting the corrie halfway. The largest drops are on the opposite side from this point, where sheer cliffs fall hundreds of feet from the grassy plateau above.

Moving alongside the edge of the corrie on initially only faint tracks, a path does, however, become more obvious and defined as it heads higher above and around the corrie. Staying on the obvious grassy path as it rises and dips along the edge of the corrie, navigation at this part of the walk is easy, and the shifting aspects of the corrie walls can be enjoyed fully until Jock's Cairn is reached at the main bluff before the next corrie, Little Corrie.

From Jock's Cairn, proceed in a southerly direction alongside the fence for approximately 500m to cross through the fence at the quad-vehicle ramp. Little Corrie comes into view here, and a route can easily be gleaned, initially traversing the edge of this smaller, less imposing corrie, and then continuing next to the cliffs for just under 1km to reach Ballagan Tops (without needing to go as far as the visible cairn). Going underfoot is often boggy in this section, as significant amounts of water drain off into Little Corrie.

The spectacular Corrie of Balglass

From the edge of the crags at Ballagan Tops the elevated ground of Earl's Seat is clearly visible in all but the worst of weather, and a short walk (a distance of 500m) over improving ground leads to the summit of Earl's Seat (578m), marked by a trig point and a cairn.

Although neither a pronounced nor entirely impressive summit, as the highest point in the Campsie Fells great views are guaranteed, and it provides the only really all-round vista on the walk. The Trossachs, Arrochar Alps and Ben Lomond rise north and west, all in magnificent contrast to the flat plain of Endrick Water. Looking south across the generally featureless interior moorland of the central Campsies, the Glasgow metropolis sprawls across the middle distance, while the Isle of Arran and Ailsa Craig are seen in the Firth of Clyde, and further behind, the Kintyre Peninsula.

The return from Earl's Seat can either retrace the original route in, or if preferred, a circular can be taken to explore the interior section of this part of the Campsies. While navigation is relatively simple for the circular suggestion that follows, it does at times involve difficult (but not impossible) terrain through heather and often boggy patches.

Go back to the fence that runs a few metres north of the trig point (which was just previously crossed) and follow it in a vaguely northeasterly direction for 800m as it moves downhill. Continue to follow it as it bends slightly where it is joined by another fence, and keep descending gradually for 600m before it kinks again, at which point it crosses a burn and then moves over more level ground for 400m.

Still staying with the fence for easy navigation, it changes direction again slightly at the intersection with another fence, and after another 400m turns at almost 90 degrees (GR592839), descending and then ascending over increasingly better ground, in a rough northerly direction for 2.4km from the right angle in the fence, to arrive back at the drystone dyke near the knoll at GR601862.

From here return easily to Fintry by the original route in via Dunmore.

WALK 27
Little Corrie and the Corrie of Balglass

Distance	11.8km
Height gain	383m
Time	3hr
Difficulty rating	4
Maps required	OS Landranger 57 (1:50,000)
	OS Explorer 348 (1:25,000)
	Harvey's Map – Glasgow Popular Hills (1:25,000)
Start point	turning for Mount Farm (GR584879)

The Corrie of Balglass and its smaller neighbour Little Corrie are easily the most impressive geological features in the Campsie Fells. This circular, looping route explores both corries, first by entering the smaller yet perhaps more atmospheric Little Corrie to gain access to the plateau above. The route then takes a path that follows the edge of Little Corrie to the high point at Jock's Cairn, before rejoining the path to manoeuvre right the way around the exhilarating rim of the Corrie of Balglass.

While a path exists for most of the walk along the top of the corries, access from the farm track into Little Corrie requires basic macro-navigation. Going underfoot is generally good apart from occasional soft ground. While in fine weather the walking on this route is spectacular without being intimidating, large drops at certain parts of the walk present a real danger on misty or windy days, which is when this walk should be avoided. (This walk is not suitable for small children or dogs.)

The walk is accessed through farmland south of the B818 at the turning for Mount Farm (GR584879), signposted with a large white placard and opposite the ruined building marked as Easter Gerchew on the map. Although once past Fintry there is no designated parking on this stretch of road, it is possible to park safely by pulling onto the widest section of grass verge approximately 30m before the Mount Farm sign.

Take the turning heading south towards Mount Farm that reaches the farm after just over 1km and a couple of right-angle turns. Go past the farm buildings and through the farmyard at the back. (As this is a working farm it is always best to ask the obliging farmer for access to the land.) Pass through the two metal gates onto the farm track that heads towards the corries.

After 600m from the farmyard turn left off the track (which leads into the forestry plantation) at GR582863 and go through the gate in the drystone dyke, entering a field normally used to graze livestock. Without a path, now head south and gradually uphill over somewhat soft but manageable ground, staying roughly parallel with the fence and the burn on the right-hand side until the perpendicular gates at GR584857 are reached. Pass over the quad ramps at the gates and continue southwesterly, still without any visible path, for approximately 500m to reach the burn that splits the main bluff between the two corries.

Now above and directly south of the forestry plantation, cross the burn and contour around the bluff, aiming to stay between the 350m and 400m contour lines, moving over more difficult, broken ground of grass and slippery, lichen-covered rocks. Cross the fence (that leads up to Jock's Cairn) then corner the bluff to receive the first views of Little Corrie. Take a route over damper ground, descending slightly, to reach the burn that bisects Little Corrie.

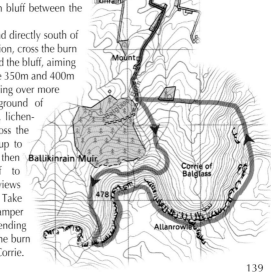

139

Little Corrie

Follow the burn as it moves further into the corrie and cross it approximately 200m before its intersection with a smaller burn, to move onto improved ground and a small spur below the crags of Snottiesneal that leads, with an increased incline, to the grassy gap between the last of the crags and the burn, an obvious and easy ramp onto the moorland plateau above Little Corrie.

Once above the corrie follow the faint quad tracks as they edge their way in an easterly direction along the lip of the corrie, gaining an excellent perspective on the shape of the corrie from midway around, until a path breaks off from the quad tracks to stay with the edge of the corrie as the quad tracks continue easterly.

Contrary to indications on the map, there is actually plenty of room for the path as it runs between the edge of the corrie and the fenceline, eventually reaching the raised ground of Jock's Cairn, where the fence is crossed to reach the small cairn, with magnificent views across Endrick Water and west towards Loch Lomond, Ben Lomond and the Arrochar Alps.

Descend from Jock's Cairn to find a vague path that again runs parallel to but some way in from the edge of the cliffs, and slowly bends round to lead onto the cliffs above the Corrie of Balglass. From here the path becomes more defined, but at certain sections it runs close to steep ground that precedes some very large but unseen drops, so a degree of caution must be exercised. ▸

The path eventually descends into a rocky cleft where the main corrie burn carves its way through the corrie wall (care should again be taken on the short scramble down to the burn). Thereafter the path rises gradually, maintaining its proximity to the edge of the corrie wall. Again, contrary to indications on the map, it is possible to stay on the path between the edge of the corrie and the nearby fence until the fence itself descends into the corrie, but those seeking less exposure should simply cross to the other side of the fence.

After completing almost three-quarters of the walk around the rim of the corrie the path peters out, and while still on easy terrain a course should be made down towards the rocky outcrop visible at the very end of the corrie's formation. Skirt easily around this outcrop and follow the obvious fence as it descends quite steeply to the drystone dyke. Pass through the gate by the dyke and follow the dyke northwards for less than 100m to where it is joined by another dyke.

At this point the dyke must be crossed, and the new dyke followed over mildly undulating terrain for a straight 1km to arrive back on the farm track opposite the forestry plantation, where the original route is taken back via the farm to the B818 to complete the walk.

This is the most exhilarating part of the walk, and it is worth stopping to admire the aerial acrobatics of ravens as they swoop and rise on updrafts rising from the corrie basin hundreds of feet below.

Jock's Cairn and Little Corrie

WALK 28
Stronend

Distance	9.8km
Height gain	411m
Time	2hr 40min
Difficulty rating	3
Maps required	OS Landranger 57 (1:50,000)
	OS Explorer 348 (1:25,000)
	Harvey's Map – Glasgow Popular Hills (1:25,000)
Start point	B818, near Fintry (GR639862)

Strictly speaking, part of the Fintry Hills rather than the Campsie Fells, the route to Stronend covers some of the most wild and remote landscape in the region, providing a unique sense of solitude and isolation. However, a lack of navigational features, potentially large drops and some difficult terrain, mean the route is as challenging as it is rewarding, and suitable only for those confident in their navigational ability.

The walk begins by crossing into fields by a cattle shed just off the B818 at GR639862, near Fintry. A lack of parking availability here may mean that for car users the walk will actually start from the nearest available parking spot, which is a small grassy lay-by opposite Gonachan Cottage (GR633862). From the cottage head back up the B818 for 750m.

On reaching the cattle shed and farm gate, cross over the stile in the drystone dyke onto the well-used farm track. Proceed immediately through the next farm gate and stay with the muddy track as it bends round. After approximately 50m (after having passed two trees on the left) cross left onto the grass, where a faint path leads up to the farm gate at the western side of the remains of Fintry Castle, the 15th-century seat of the Grahams of Fintry.

Moving through the farm gate an impressive set of crags and a small waterfall soon come into view. Continue gradually uphill on the well-used and rutted farm tracks, moving to the right of the crags and arriving at a stile in a fence just to the left of the Spout of Balbowie. Use the stile to cross over the fence next to the sheep fold and proceed over the stile in the next fence.

The farm vehicle tracks continue to head uphill from this point and should be followed for another 300m, running parallel to the burn, to reach another gate with a stile next to it. Once over this fence the conditions underfoot noticeably change to rougher moorland terrain. Any signs of a path or vehicle tracks also disappear, making accurate navigation immediately more important.

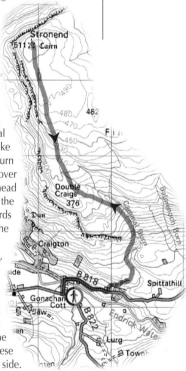

Continue to ascend gradually over the increasingly tussocky but manageable terrain for just under 1km, all the time keeping the Cammal Burn near on the right-hand side. The burn acts as a useful navigational handrail until a small drystone dyke is reached, just near where the burn begins to bend northwards. Cross over the dyke and change direction to head northwards, still staying parallel to the narrowing burn, and moving towards the steep but small bank close to the source of the burn.

Once up and over the bank, navigation becomes more difficult, as do the conditions underfoot. Still heading northwards towards the cairn at Stronend, it is now best to switch to using the edge of the crags as the navigational handrail, keeping these a healthy distance on the left-hand side.

...ng light over Fintry and Stronend

Attention should be paid to using this technique in poor visibility, as straying too close to the crags could be disastrous. The terrain over this section towards the cairn is particularly soft and boggy in parts, and choosing the best route through the boggier areas can easily interrupt efforts to navigate. A number of well-concealed drainage ditches are an additional hazard.

The ground continues to rise very gently until the high point at Stronend (511m), which is marked with a large stone shelter around a very old-looking triangulation point. The best views here are to the north and west, where already spectacular panoramas are made even more dramatic as the cliffs fall away sharply towards the flat arable fields directly below.

Returning by exactly the same route taken in is almost impossible, and departing from the summit presents further navigational complications, as there is much less (in terms of navigational attack points) to aim for. It should be noted that even in good visibility, on leaving the summit of Stronend it is easy to stray into the featureless and disorientating ground to the east. Try to head back towards the crags, again safely using them as a handrail on the way back, but this time on the right-hand side, returning to the Cammal Burn and the dyke and the route off the hill.

The Double Craigs en route to Stronend

WALK 29
North Third Reservoir Walk

Distance	8.9km
Height gain	230m
Time	2hr 10min
Difficulty rating	3
Maps required	OS Landranger 57 (1:50,000)
	OS Explorer 348 (1:25,000)
Start point	southern edge of North Third Reservoir (GR758879)

Situated in a little-known corner of central Scotland, but neither wholly part of the Campsie Fells or the Ochils, this undemanding walk fully justifies its inclusion because of some unique scenery and a wide diversity of flora and fauna.

After an initial easy climb above North Third Reservoir to Lewis Hill and the remarkable Sauchie Craigs, the route becomes a figure-of-eight forest walk that includes a Site of Special Scientific Interest as well as several interesting historic and natural features. The combination of natural woodland, forestry plantations and the reservoir means this is also an excellent area to spot wildlife.

There are good paths and forest tracks throughout the walk, but also occasional sections where paths are at the edge of large drops on Sauchie Craigs, making parts of this route potentially unsuitable for those with with small children or dogs.

The walk begins at GR758879 by woodland at the southern edge of North Third Reservoir, where space is available for several cars to park.

Take the established path that runs alongside the mixed woodland of beech, pine and oak trees, avoiding any paths that veer into the woodland itself, instead keeping the fence and cleared forestry on the right-hand side. Within about five minutes the wood becomes more coniferous, and the ground steepens for a brief period as the obvious path bends around and behind the southern end of the crags, coming into more open ground on the top.

Once on the level plateau of the crags, views immediately open up, with the first excellent vantage point gained on a large round boulder next to a solitary tree, where there is one of the best views down to the several densely wooded islands on the reservoir.

Continue along the path in a northerly direction to reach the triangulation point of Lewis Hill (266m), where good views extend north and west to the Trossachs, Ben Vorlich and Ben Chonzie, as well as the Ochils close by in the east. Stay with the path as it gently rises and dips over good ground, passing the barely distinguishable site of an Iron Age fort to the left, as well as some stunning rock formations and columns on the crags.

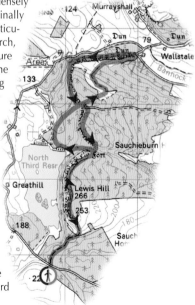

The path then begins to descend more steeply on a switchback path to the densely wooded Windy Yet Glen (originally meaning 'windy gate'), which is particularly colourful in autumn, when birch, rowan, beech and oak display a mixture of different hues. At the bottom of the glen the path forks by a waymarking post with a yellow arrow – take the left-hand fork, passing through coniferous trees with glimpses of the cliffs above, to soon arrive at the edge of the reservoir wall.

At this point another waymarking post is visible, indicating the obvious path that runs just below the reservoir fence until a black iron gate is reached at the corner of the fence. Instead of following the fenceline from the iron gate, head back into the forestry plantation along the path at the wide firebreak, as indicated by the third waymarking post.

The view down to North Third Reservoir

The broad path now continues for some 700m through the firebreak before bending round as it ascends, just after a small clearing in the trees allows glimpses of the crags once more. Stay on this now-established forestry track (ignoring any less-defined options to turn off it), heading in a generally northeasterly direction and gradually descending until some double wooden gates are reached.

Pass by the gates and turn left onto a more established track that runs parallel with Bannock Burn, passing a large white house and entering some woodland where the track bends sharply. Leave the track at the bend and head directly onwards now, on a path that leads into a fine, predominantly ash woodland.

Currently a Site of Special Scientific Interest, this unusual wood thrives on a limestone-rich base, which is also the reason for the presence of the early purple orchid, which flowers from April through to late June. Five minutes after entering the wood, where the path forks, the large, vegetated stone structures on the right-hand side are the remains of massive limekilns, originally used over 150 years ago to extract lime by smelting the nearby limestone in huge furnaces. The lime was then used for improving the soil of the neighbouring farmlands.

The path continues pleasantly through the ash wood, running alongside Bannock Burn for a while before gradually regaining some height and re-entering a dense conifer plantation. Here the path eventually rejoins the large forest track at the small clearing previously visited. From here, head in the same direction as before (northeast and away from the reservoir), straightaway moving up the sloping bend in the track, this time taking the first right-hand path off the track, and then immediately afterwards taking another less obvious right-hand path.

This smaller path rises briefly and enters into more mixed woodland to run along the edge of the crags, where attention should be paid, as there are some large drops in places. The path continues as an exhilarating walk along the edge of the cliff, over changing terrain for about 10 minutes, until it reaches the established path that doubles back to descend back into Windy Yet Glen, thus completing the figure-of-eight part of the walk.

Once in the small glen the path leads back to the familiar waymarking post at the fork in the path. From here the original path back up and out of the glen can be taken, leading back to Lewis Hill and the start of the walk.

The spectacular Sauchie Craig below Lewis Hill

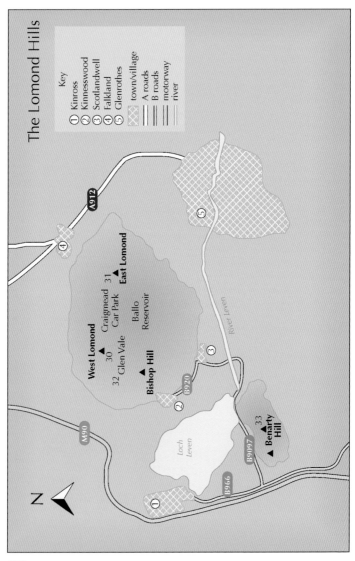

The Lomond Hills

Key

① Kinross
② Kinnesswood
③ Scotlandwell
④ Falkland
⑤ Glenrothes

town/village
A roads
B roads
motorway
river

A912

West Lomond
30
32 Glen Vale
Bishop Hill

Craigmead 31
Car Park
East Lomond
Ballo
Reservoir

River Leven

B920
③

②

M90

Loch
Leven

①

B9097

33
Benarty
Hill

B966

N

THE LOMOND HILLS

Viewed from the M90 motorway the Lomond Hills appear deceptively larger than their actual height, and present an enticing and intriguing profile. The well-defined shape of West Lomond (**Walk 32**) is the focal point for the range as it towers above expansive Loch Leven, but a closer inspection of the hills reveals other notable areas of interest, in particular the sheer crags of the Benarty Hill Ridge (**Walk 33**) on the opposite side of the loch and the impressive dolerite crags and columns under Bishops Hill. The peak of East Lomond (**Walk 31**), although slightly lower than its twin, West Lomond, is similarly well defined in shape and worthy of a visit. The range is best experienced by walking the almost circular route around the plateau **(Walk 30)**, although it is easy to access short walks to either East or West Lomond from the car park at Craigmead.

The area also includes several less obvious features deserving of exploration, such as narrow Glen Vale (**Walk 32**), the nearby, bizzarely shaped sandstone formation of the Bonnet Stane, and the impressive historical sites of Falkland Palace and Falkland Estate.

View across Loch Leven (Walk 33)

WALK 30
The Lomond Circuit

Distance	13.9km
Height gain	472m
Time	3hr 30min
Difficulty rating	3
Maps required	OS Landranger 58 (1:50,000)
	OS Explorer 369 (1:25,000)
Start point	Craigmead car park (GR227063)

This popular circular walk takes in the full character of the Lomond Hills, including several of the most interesting features in the range, such as Glen Vale and the freestanding dolerite stack known as Carlin Maggie, as well as the highest peak, West Lomond (522m). With the exception of one short section, well-established paths, tracks and roads exist throughout the walk, making navigation uncomplicated and the going underfoot generally good.

The walk starts and finishes at the Craigmead car park at GR227063, west of Falkland. This large car park is an indication of the popularity of walks in the Lomond Hills, and is well situated for access to both East and West Lomond, as well as the nearby Ballo Reservoir.

Begin the walk from the back of the car park, taking the path through the scattering of Scots pines to arrive on open ground after crossing a stile in the fence. A very obvious grassy path moves diagonally towards a broad vehicle track, built to access Wilkie's Quarry, but now providing a direct but aesthetically harsh route for a distance of just under 3km to the base of West Lomond. Grassy banks to the right also mean views from the track are limited on this flat and rather uninteresting start to the walk. However, as West Lomond draws closer, more rewarding views north are visible and the scenery begins to improve.

On reaching the base of West Lomond after passing by the ugly gouges of the quarry, take the obvious footpath that forks left from the track and zigzags steeply up the northeastern side of the hill, to arrive without too much effort on the rather jumbled summit of West Lomond (522m), marked not only by a triangulation point but also a large cairn and several makeshift stone windbreaks.

> The isolation of the Lomond Hills rising above the level farmland below means that views from this, the largest Lomond summit, do not disappoint. To the north the southerly reaches of the Cairngoms are often visible in winter as a white, snow-covered band on the horizon. The cities of Perth and Dundee are also visible in the north on different sections of the River Tay. To the west, as height is lost dramatically from the eastern slopes, the true 'island' character of the Lomond Hills becomes apparent, as the Ochils are the only other significant rise in gradient in the middle distance. To the south and east the land gradually slopes less dramatically past the reservoirs into a more rural expanse.

The gradual slope up West Lomond with East Lomond in the distance

Numerous paths meet at West Lomond summit, but a vaguely southerly path should be taken to eventually arrive at the track at the head of Glen Vale. Descending quite steep ground initially, cross a fence by a drystone dyke to enter into a rough area that is the only section of the walk that lacks any paths. The same direction should be maintained across patches of heather of approximately 700m to reach the increasingly obvious fence by the track on the other side of Glen Vale. On reaching the top of Glen Vale an interesting detour is provided by the narrow path to the right that heads down Glen Vale to the small outcrop known locally as John Knox's Pulpit, and past several interesting water features along the burn.

From the track cross through the gate and proceed south next to the low drystone dyke, gradually moving uphill for 400m until a gap is reached in the dyke next to a wooden fence. At this point take the footpath that heads off the track at a right angle in a westwards direction. This path continues for just under 1km, over fairly good ground, until it bends at a right angle again as it reaches the edge of the eastern slopes, from where spectacular views over the huge expanse of Loch Leven can be enjoyed.

Now heading south, still on the obvious path, the highest point on Bishop Hill, a small knoll, is soon passed on the left.

Just after this point a detour right over the fence leads to one of the most interesting features in the Lomonds, a section of interesting quartz dolerite outcrop, including the large freestanding stack known locally as Carlin Maggie, which is occasionally attempted by climbers. **Attention is required** reaching this outcrop as the slopes are quite steep in parts.

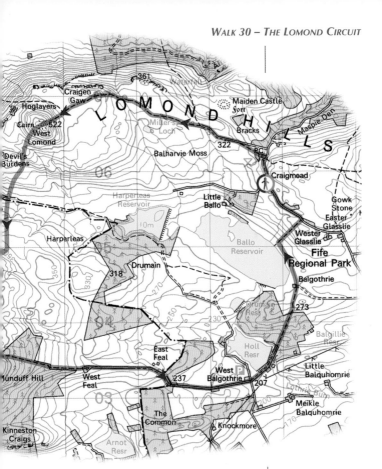

The path continues around, moving away from the edge of the plateau, eventually arriving at the stile at the edge of the plantation on Munduff Hill. From here navigation is straightforward as tracks and roads connect, heading eastwards and gradually descending into more agricultural land, passing West Feal Farm, East Feal, and eventually arriving at the cross-roads by West Balgothrie.

Go straight across at the junction, following the

155

signposts for Craigmead, and pass Holl Reservoir on the left and the processing plant on the right to arrive at a bridge with blue railings. Cross the bridge and proceed into the forestry plantation, now leaving the road and walking on a distinct but at times boggy path through the forest firebreak. Open farmland is soon re-entered and the path becomes very muddy in parts.

Before Balgothrie is reached a signpost to Craigmead gives clear direction that the path heads down towards Ballo Reservoir. The path then follows the edge of the reservoir for a few hundred metres to arrive at a stile by a tarmac road near a building. Cross this stile, then the stile opposite, and follow the path as indicated by the white arrow on the signpost.

The path bends round at a right angle and heads uphill, with a fence on the left-hand side, towards a small cluster of trees, after which the road comes into view. This is a good vantage point to look back and retrace the route taken so far, and is also the best view across the reservoirs. On reaching the road, turn left and continue along it for 1km to return to the car park at Craigmead.

The dolerite column of Carlin Maggie below Bishop's Hill

WALK 31
East Lomond Circuit

Distance	8.9km
Height gain	349m
Time	2hr 30min
Difficulty rating	3
Maps required	OS Landranger 58 (1:50,000)
	OS Landranger 59 (1:50,000)
	OS Explorer 370 (1:25,000)
Start point	Craigmead car park (GR227063)

Set around the historic town of Falkland, this relatively undemanding circular walk takes in marvellous and easily accessible views from East Lomond (424m), as well as exploring many interesting historical features scattered around the Falkland Estate. The route links up several paths, vehicle tracks and roads, ensuring that navigation is simple and going underfoot is good.

Starting from the ever-busy Craigmead car park at GR227063, west of Falkland, head out of the car park entrance and cross the road to a vehicle track almost directly opposite the entrance. Head uphill initially on this well-established track, before the ground evens out onto flat moorland, with East Lomond rising directly in the east and fine views north and back to West Lomond. Stay on the track for 1km before crossing through a brown gate on the left and following the grassy footpath that leads directly and with increasing steepness to the summit of East Lomond (424m).

The focus of the small, flat summit is the newly erected direction finder, a useful addition to a hill with such good all-round views. The best views are northwards, where

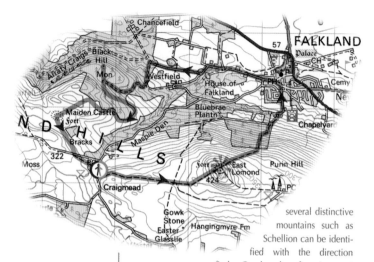

several distinctive mountains such as Schellion can be identified with the direction finder. On clear days, fine views east across Fife and out towards the North Sea are also enjoyed. The summit also bears evidence of its previous use as an Iron Age fort, which can be seen to encircle almost the entire summit.

Leave the summit on the path that heads northeasterly towards the stile in the fence (this steep descent can be made more gradual by initially heading east of the summit and then following the fence around to the stile). Once through the stile stay on the obvious path, which leads into a coniferous plantation and then a marvellous beech woodland before arriving at a vehicle track after a series of steps.

Turn right at the vehicle track and shortly arrive at the end of a street next to a large factory which is at the south end of Falkland. Head downhill along this road to arrive at the fountain by Falkland Parish Church near Falkland Palace, of which both beautiful buildings deserve closer inspection.

From the road by the fountain turn left, and continue in a westwards direction for 200m until the road bends at a right angle and proceeds uphill. Instead of following the main road as it bends, continue on the narrower road straight ahead, marked with a sign pointing to a golf course. This road soon arrives at the grand gatehouse of the Falkland Estate. ▶

Continue along the main estate road, still heading in a westerly direction until the road splits in three. Take the middle track and turn left, just opposite playing fields, as this road bends. Approximately 30m up the road from the bend, take the turning right into a small copse, which shortly after runs onto a straight and very pleasant hedge-lined vehicle track. Stay on this track until the forest plantation is reached and pass through a metal archway immediately after entering the plantation.

Once through the archway turn immediately and sharply left and proceed uphill on a soft track for 200m to arrive at an established track for forestry vehicles. Turn right on reaching this track and stay on it for 10 minutes as it loops and bends upwards, reaching an obvious fork after a long curving section. As another interesting diversion take the right-hand fork and follow the path over slightly boggier ground to quickly reach the Tyndall Bruce monument, soon visible through the trees. The conspicuous and solitary monument provides a fine vantage point through the trees to the north of Fife.

After entering the estate a useful information board on the right gives details of the estate, while opposite and to the left a path leads up to a magnificent ruined mausoleum, which is certainly worth a detour to see.

Evening sun on East Lomond

East Lomond

Turn right at the fork and continue to head uphill. Stay with the track as it ascends through loops and bends to eventually arrive at more open ground that provides fine views across to East Lomond. The track ends, but a small and obvious footpath leads on into increasingly open ground to reach a stile in a fence at the edge of the forestry.

Cross the stile and turn right, now without a path, following the fenceline uphill slightly as it leads around the top edge of the forestry, passing a younger woodland regeneration scheme. Stay next to the forestry fence, walking through some heather to reach the corner of the forestry on Green Hill (GR225072).

From the corner of the forestry head southwesterly, initially walking upwards onto the knoll marked as 314m on the map, and then continue to the obvious raised ground of Maiden Castle Fort, an impressive example of an Iron Age fort. From the fort head southeasterly across to the small copse of pines, passing them on their south side to find a small path that becomes more defined as it continues southeasterly towards the vehicle track and drystone dyke.

As the path emerges at the track, cross through the gap in the dyke to enter onto a path on short grass that heads directly back to the Craigmead car park, thus completing the walk.

WALK 32
Glen Vale and West Lomond

Distance	9.1km
Height gain	362m
Time	2hr 20min
Difficulty rating	2
Maps required	OS Landranger 58 (1:50,000)
	OS Explorer 370 (1:25,000)
Start point	car park (GR173069)

This interesting circular route starts by heading up picturesque Glen Vale, passing the sandstone outcrop and historic site of Presbyterian conventicles, known as John Knox's Pulpit, before rising to the summit of West Lomond and returning by the remarkable, mushroom-shaped geological feature of the Bonnet Stane. Paths exists for most of this walk, except for the relatively short middle section, where some fairly easy route finding over heather and tussocked grass is required.

From the small village of Glenlomond head northwards on the Dryside Road, passing the Muirs of Kinnesswood (1:25,000 map), to reach the car park at GR173069. Leave the car park and turn left, entering a small copse after 200m. In the copse take the path over the stile signposted as 'Footpath to Glen Vale'.

The well-established footpath proceeds in a southeasterly direction next to Glen Burn for almost 2km before entering into the steeper-sided Glen Vale. A large outcrop soon comes into view on the left. Known as John Knox's Pulpit, it is so called because it was supposedly the secret meeting place for supporters of the Reformation. Continuing along the path, the burn runs further below as the narrow cleft of the glen becomes steeper. ▶

At this point the gouging effect of the water can be seen as several small caves are visible on the opposite side of the burn, formed presumably by eddies many thousands of years ago when the water was at a much higher level than today.

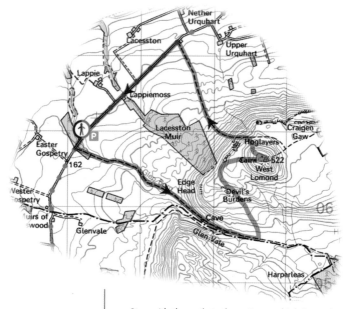

As the highest peak in the Lomond Hills, spectacular and unimpeded views stretch out in every direction, most notably west to the Ochils, north to the Cairngorms, and east out into the North Sea.

Stay with the path to the point at which it reaches a vehicle track at GR194056, just opposite a gate on the other side of the burn. Leave the path now and head directly north through heather in the direction of the small rocky bank known as the Devil's Burdens. The route finding and going underfoot on this short section are quite difficult, but on reaching the boulders beneath the Devil's Burdens the ground improves.

From here head in a roughly northwesterly direction, still without a path, towards the edge of the escarpment. On reaching the escarpment, and with fine views west, proceed alongside the steep slope in a northeasterly direction to reach a fence near the spot-height 429m. Cross over the fence, and with the slope of West Lomond now in full view, begin to ascend the well-worn path up the side of the final steep section of West Lomond, to reach the trig point and numerous cairns on the summit (522m). ◀

The Bonnet Stane
© George Lupton

Leave the summit by means of the same final path used for the ascent, and stay with this path as it bends at almost a right angle and continues to contour around the top slope of West Lomond. Instead of moving around the hill, though, descend northwards without a path a for approximately 100m to join the path that descends past the area marked as 'Hoglayers' on the map (Explorer).

This path descends steeply through a narrow cleft before levelling out, and crosses a fence by means of a fixed ladder. The path then passes the single most interesting geological feature in the range, the Bonnet Stane.

> The Bonnet Stone is a large sandstone mass rising incongruously out of the flat field, with a distinctive large tabletop 'bonnet' that rests on a narrow neck of rock. There is also a cave that has been carved out of the sandstone, which according to local legend was the home of a female hermit, driven to live there after the death of her lover.

From the Bonnet Stone continue to head northwesterly to the middle edge of the field, where a gap in the dyke leads to a broad vehicle track, marked on the map, that runs parallel to the fence until it reaches the car park at GR185081.

On reaching the road and the car park turn left, and it is a simple case of walking back along the quiet road for just over 1.5km to return to the original car park.

WALK 33
Benarty Hill Ridge

Distance	7km
Height gain	197m
Time	1hr 40min
Difficulty rating	2
Maps required	OS Landranger 58 (1:50,000)
	OS Explorer 367 (1:25,000)
	OS Explorer 369 (1:25,000)
	OS Explorer 370 (1:25,000)
Start point	car park, Vane Farm Nature Reserve (GR159991)

Separate from the largest bulk of the Lomond Hills, Benarty Hill and its ridge lie on the south side of Scotland's largest lowland loch, Loch Leven, and are easily identified (and accessed) from the M90 motorway by their dramatic northern escarpment and large dolerite crags. Although this route is not circular, it starts and finishes from the nature reserve at Vane Farm, thus providing an ideal opportunity to enjoy fine walking with excellent views across one of the country's most important habitats for migrating birds and wildfowl. The walk follows visible paths for most of the way, although for a substantial section of the route on top of the ridge the path lies amongst heather.

Start from the large car park at Vane Farm Nature Reserve, just off the B9097 and south of Loch Leven (GR159991). From the car park go through the large gate and round past the opposite side of the visitor centre, to encounter two signposted routes at the bottom of a small, open, grassy area. Take the left-hand route, marked 'Viewpoint'.

The established path soon leads upwards through pleasant birch woodland, which is particularly active with birdlife in spring and summer, and soon passes a

bench with a fine viewpoint across Loch Leven. Approximately 200m further uphill, take the left-hand route as the path forks.

Vane Farm nature reserve and Loch Leven

The path then moves up and above the woodland before switching direction to contour around the hill, with impressive views ahead of West Lomond, after which it ascends again to shortly arrive at the spectacular viewpoint of Vane Hill (253m).

From the hill, views stretch down across the wetlands of the nature reserve and the huge expanse of Loch Leven. The largest island visible on the loch, St Serfs, is an important breeding ground for wildfowl and a nesting site for migrating geese, but was previously inhabited by priors of the Augustinian Order. The ruins of the 9th-century priory are still visible on the island today. Further west on the loch, Castle Island and the now ruined Loch Leven Castle were the infamous place of captivity for Mary Queen of Scots, who was imprisoned here for a year until she effected an elaborate and daring escape in 1568.

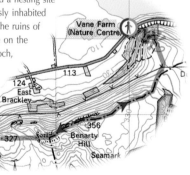

West Lomond and Loch Leven from the Benarty Hill Ridge

From Vane Hill leave the obvious path and follow the faint path that runs south, parallel to the fence and drystone dyke. As the path fades, stay next to the dyke until the corner is reached near a pylon approximately 100m from the viewpoint.

At this point cross over the dyke and fence into the neighbouring field. Now on short grass, cross the field diagonally in a southwesterly direction towards the corner of the Egg Forestry Plantation, aiming for two obvious Scots pines just to the left of some small outcrops. The noticeable dips passed in this field are the result of quarrying.

Once at the Scots pines, head directly up the bank to reach a plateaued area covered with heather. Move around to the right, walking above the small crags, and cross over the fence into the heather. The narrow but established path that is visible in amongst the heather, running parallel to the fence, should be taken in a roughly westerly direction along the Benarty Hill ridge. The going underfoot can at times be tricky, as heather constantly brushes feet and ankles, but after a while the heather recedes and the path becomes more established on short grass, leading to the summit of Benarty Hill (356m), marked with a trig point. ▶

From the trig point continue along the obvious path, dropping down past the site of what is probably an Iron Age fort on the left, and proceed uphill onto the small ridge that curves around towards the unnamed spot-height (327m) above the crags at the western end of Benarty Hill Ridge. **Attention must be paid not to stray further west into the area used as a rifle range**.

It is possible to make this route circular by descending from the ridge at the shallowest incline near the Iron Age fort and continuing on the flatter ground below the impressive dolerite crags, eventually rejoining the established path in the nature reserve. However, the terrain in parts is tricky, with several fences to negotiate, and the recommended route is to retrace the inward path back along the ridge, this time enjoying fine eastward views.

The best views here are gained away from the trig point by crossing to the other side of the fence, from where West Lomond is prominent in the immediate north and a large stretch of the Ochils are visible in the west.

167

A light dusting of snow over the Grodwell Burn (Walk 11)

APPENDIX:
Further Information

Outdoor Access Code
www.outdooraccess-scotland.com

Ochils Mountain Rescue
www.mrc-scotland.org.uk/ochils

Lomond Mountain Rescue
www.mrc-scotland.org.uk/lomond

Scottish Natural Heritage
www.snh.org.uk

Woodland Trust
www.woodland-trust.org.uk

Forestry Commission Scotland
Silvan House
231 Corstorphine Road
Edinburgh
EH12 7AT
Tel: 0131 334 0303
Fax: 0131 314 6152
www.forestry.gov.uk/scotland

Area Guides
www.undiscoveredscotland.co.uk
www.visitscottishheartlands.com
www.kilsyth.org.uk/Environment/kilsyth_hills

Useful Books
Central Scotland: Land, Wildlife, People, L. Corbett, ed. (The Forth Naturalist and Historian, 2005, ISBN 1 89800 800 0)
Mountaincraft and Leadership, Eric Langmuir (Scottish Sports Council – SportScotland, 1995, ISBN 1 85060 295 6)
The Hillwalker's Manual, Bill Birkett (Cicerone Press, 2002, ISBN 1 85284 341 1)

NOTES

NOTES

LISTING OF CICERONE GUIDES

BACKPACKING
Backpacker's Britain Vol 1 –
   Northern England
Backpacker's Britain Vol 2 – Wales
Backpacker's Britain Vol 3 –
   Northern Scotland
Book of the Bivvy
End to End Trail
Three Peaks, Ten Tors

BRITISH CYCLE GUIDES
Border Country Cycle Routes
Cumbria Cycle Way
Lancashire Cycle Way
Lands End to John O'Groats –
   Cycle Guide
Rural Rides No.1 – West Surrey
Rural Rides No.2 – East Surrey
South Lakeland Cycle Rides

CANOE GUIDES
Canoeist's Guide to the North-East

**DERBYSHIRE, PEAK DISTRICT,
EAST MIDLANDS**
High Peak Walks
Historic Walks in Derbyshire
Star Family Walks Peak District and
   South Yorkshire
White Peak Walks Northern Dales
White Peak Walks Southern Dales

FOR COLLECTORS OF SUMMITS
Mts England & Wales Vol 1 – Wales
Mts England & Wales Vol 2 –
   England
Relative Hills of Britain

IRELAND
Irish Coast to Coast
Irish Coastal Walks
Mountains of Ireland

ISLE OF MAN
Isle of Man Coastal Path
Walking on the Isle of Man

**LAKE DISTRICT AND
MORECAMBE BAY**
Atlas of the English Lakes
Coniston Copper Mines
Cumbria Coastal Way
Cumbria Way and Allerdale Ramble
Great Mountain Days in the
   Lake District
Lake District Angler's Guide
Lake District Winter Climbs
Roads and Tracks of the Lake
   District
Rocky Rambler's Wild Walks
Scrambles in the Lake District
   (North)
Scrambles in the Lake District
   (South)
Short Walks in Lakeland 1 – South
Short Walks in Lakeland 2 – North
Short Walks in Lakeland 3 – West
Tarns of Lakeland Vol 1 – West
Tarns of Lakeland Vol 2 – East

Tour of the Lake District
Walks in Silverdale and
   Arnside AONB

MIDLANDS
Cotswold Way

**NORTHERN ENGLAND
LONG-DISTANCE TRAILS**
Dales Way
Hadrian's Wall Path
Northern Coast to Coast Walk
Pennine Way
Teesdale Way

NORTH-WEST ENGLAND
Family Walks in the
   Forest of Bowland
Historic Walks in Cheshire
Ribble Way
Walker's Guide to the
   Lancaster Canal
Walking in the Forest of Bowland
   and Pendle
Walking in Lancashire
Walks in Lancashire Witch Country
Walks in Ribble Country

**PENNINES AND
NORTH-EAST ENGLAND**
Cleveland Way and Yorkshire
   Wolds Way
Historic Walks in North Yorkshire
North York Moors
South Pennine Walks
Yorkshire Dales – South and West
Walking in County Durham
Walking in the North Pennines
Walking in Northumberland
Walking in the South Pennines
Walking in the Wolds
Walks in Dales Country
Walks in the Yorkshire Dales
Walks on the North York Moors,
   books 1 and 2
Waterfall Walks – Teesdale and
   High Pennines
Yorkshire Dales Angler's Guide

SCOTLAND
Ben Nevis and Glen Coe
Border Country – A Walker's Guide
Border Pubs and Inns –
   A Walkers' Guide
Central Highlands: 6 Long
   Distance Walks
Great Glen Way
Isle of Skye, A Walker's Guide
North to the Cape
Pentland Hills: A Walker's Guide
Scotland's Far North
Scotland's Far West
Scotland's Mountain Ridges
Scottish Glens 1 – Cairngorm Glens
Scottish Glens 2 – Atholl Glens
Scottish Glens 3 – Glens of
   Rannoch

Scottish Glens 4 – Glens of
   Trossach
Scottish Glens 5 – Glens of Argyll
Scottish Glens 6 – The Great Glen
Scrambles in Lochaber
Southern Upland Way
Torridon – A Walker's Guide
Walking in the Cairngorms
Walking in the Hebrides
Walking in the Isle of Arran
Walking in the Lowther Hills
Walking in the Ochils, Campsie
   Fells and Lomond Hills
Walking the Galloway Hills
Walking the Munros Vol 1 –
   Southern, Central
Walking the Munros Vol 2 –
   Northern and Cairngorms
West Highland Way
Winter Climbs – Ben Nevis and
   Glencoe
Winter Climbs – Cairngorms

SOUTHERN ENGLAND
Channel Island Walks
Definitive Guide to Walking
   in London
Exmoor and the Quantocks
Greater Ridgeway
Isles of Scilly
Lea Valley Walk
North Downs Way
South Downs Way
South West Coast Path
Thames Path
Walker's Guide to the Isle of Wight
Walking in Bedfordshire
Walking in Berkshire
Walking in Buckinghamshire
Walking in Dorset
Walking in Kent
Walking in Somerset
Walking in Sussex
Walking on Dartmoor

UK GENERAL
National Trails

WALES AND WELSH BORDERS
Ascent of Snowdon
Glyndwr's Way
Hillwalking in Wales – Vol 1
Hillwalking in Wales – Vol 2
Hillwalking in Snowdonia
Lleyn Peninsula Coastal Path
Pembrokeshire Coastal Path
Ridges of Snowdonia
Scrambles in Snowdonia
Shropshire Hills – A Walker's Guide
Spirit Paths of Wales
Walking Offa's Dyke Path
Walking in Pembrokeshire
Welsh Winter Climbs

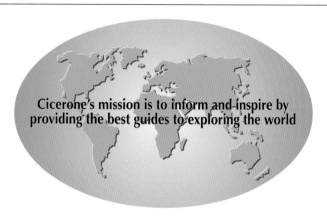

Cicerone's mission is to inform and inspire by providing the best guides to exploring the world

Since its foundation over 30 years ago, Cicerone has specialised in publishing guidebooks and has built a reputation for quality and reliability. It now publishes nearly 300 guides to the major destinations for outdoor enthusiasts, including Europe, UK and the rest of the world.

Written by leading and committed specialists, Cicerone guides are recognised as the most authoritative. They are full of information, maps and illustrations so that the user can plan and complete a successful and safe trip or expedition – be it a long face climb, a walk over Lakeland fells, an alpine traverse, a Himalayan trek or a ramble in the countryside.

With a thorough introduction to assist planning, clear diagrams, maps and colour photographs to illustrate the terrain and route, and accurate and detailed text, Cicerone guides are designed for ease of use and access to the information.

If the facts on the ground change, or there is any aspect of a guide that you think we can improve, we are always delighted to hear from you.

Cicerone Press
2 Police Square Milnthorpe Cumbria LA7 7PY
Tel:01539 562 069   Fax:01539 563 417
e-mail:info@cicerone.co.uk   web:www.cicerone.co.uk

CICERONE